AF498236

KRISTEN PARKER

The Last Dawn of Winter's Embrace

Copyright © 2025 by Kristen Parker

All rights reserved. No part of this publication may be reproduced, stored or transmitted in any form or by any means, electronic, mechanical, photocopying, recording, scanning, or otherwise without written permission from the publisher. It is illegal to copy this book, post it to a website, or distribute it by any other means without permission.

This novel is entirely a work of fiction. The names, characters and incidents portrayed in it are the work of the author's imagination. Any resemblance to actual persons, living or dead, events or localities is entirely coincidental.

Kristen Parker asserts the moral right to be identified as the author of this work.

Kristen Parker has no responsibility for the persistence or accuracy of URLs for external or third-party Internet Websites referred to in this publication and does not guarantee that any content on such Websites is, or will remain, accurate or appropriate.

Designations used by companies to distinguish their products are often claimed as trademarks. All brand names and product names used in this book and on its cover are trade names, service marks, trademarks and registered trademarks of their respective owners. The publishers and the book are not associated with any product or vendor mentioned in this book. None of the companies referenced within the book have endorsed the book.

First edition

This book was professionally typeset on Reedsy.
Find out more at reedsy.com

Contents

1 The Eternal Night 1

2 Frost and Fire 12

3 The Queen's Command 23

4 The Forbidden Touch 34

5 Secrets Beneath the Ice 45

6 The Frostbite of Betrayal 56

7 Heart of Ice 67

8 Ice In The Heart 79

9 The Weight of the Frost 90

10 The Shattered Crown 101

11 The First Flame 112

12 The Breaking of Winter 125

13 The Last Dawn 135

14 The Fire and the Ice 147

15 The Price of Sacrifice 158

16 The War of the Seasons 169

17 The Last Embrace 180

18 The Dawn of Spring 191

19 The Return of the Moon 201

20 The Last Winter's Embrace 211

21 The Final Dawn 222

One

The Eternal Night

The wind howled through the streets of the capital city of Amara, carrying with it the icy bite of a winter that had no end. The kingdom was locked in an eternal night, the sun a mere myth, a distant memory that had long since faded into the shadows. The people lived in this perpetual winter, their lives defined by the frozen landscape that stretched endlessly before them. In the streets, the snow piled high, never melting, and the chill in the air cut through even the thickest of cloaks. The world was cold, unyielding, and inescapable. Yet amidst the endless frost, there was one figure who embodied the true weight of the season—the Winter Queen, Ysra.

Ysra's power was absolute, her command over the cold unchallenged. The snow did not fall without her permission, and the chill of the air was her doing. The people of Amara spoke of her with both reverence and fear, for her rule was as unrelenting as the winter itself. She kept the kingdom frozen in time, ensuring that no warmth would ever again touch the land. And so it was that Lira, a young woman of the Queen's guard, stood beneath the shadow of the Queen's palace, her breath visible in the air as she gazed out over the city. The lights of the capital twinkled faintly in the distance, but even they seemed dimmed by the weight of the eternal night.

Lira had been raised in this world, where the cold was more than just a season—it was a way of life. She had never known anything different. Her childhood had been filled with the biting winds and the heavy snows that had blanketed the kingdom for as long as anyone could remember. It was the only world she knew. And it was a world she had sworn to protect.

As a member of the Queen's guard, Lira's duty was clear: to serve the Queen, to uphold her laws, and to ensure that the frost of the kingdom's rule never thawed. She had never questioned her role, never wavered in her devotion to the Queen's cause. But there were moments—brief, fleeting moments—when something stirred inside her. A flicker of doubt, a whisper of something warmer that she couldn't quite grasp. It was in the quiet of the night, when she stood alone in the palace corridors, her mind racing with thoughts she dared not voice. There was something she was meant to understand, something that lay hidden beneath the surface of her life, something that could shatter the very world she had sworn to protect.

A prophecy, whispered in the coldest of nights, haunted her thoughts.

They said that love would break the eternal winter. A forbidden love, one that would tear through the frost like a flame through the ice. A love that could undo the very curse that bound the kingdom in its endless chill. It was a tale told in hushed voices, a secret passed between the oldest of the kingdom's elders. Lira had heard it as a child, a story that had seemed like nothing more than a fairytale—a myth to pass the time on long, cold nights. But now, as she stood beneath the frozen sky, the weight of the words felt more like a warning than a story.

The queen's reign had lasted for centuries, and the curse of eternal winter had been cast long ago, an act of sacrifice that kept something darker at bay. But what if the prophecy was true? What if love could truly shatter the frost, end the endless night, and bring warmth back to the world? What if, in the depths of the coldest night, Lira had been chosen to fulfill that prophecy?

The thought was a dangerous one. Lira knew it. And yet, she could not shake the feeling that something was changing. That something was coming.

Her thoughts were interrupted by the sound of footsteps behind her. She turned quickly, her hand instinctively reaching for the hilt of her sword. But it was not an enemy that stood before her—it was her fellow guard, Aric. His broad shoulders were hunched against the cold, his face obscured by the fur-lined hood of his cloak.

"Lira," he said, his voice low and grave. "The Queen demands your presence. Now."

Lira hesitated for only a moment before nodding. "I'll be there."

Aric's eyes lingered on her for a moment longer than necessary, as though he could sense the turmoil within her. But he said nothing more, turning on his heel and walking back toward the palace. Lira followed, her boots crunching in the snow as she moved through the city, her mind still racing with the whispers of the prophecy.

The palace loomed ahead, a massive structure of stone and ice, its towers rising into the sky like jagged teeth. The air around it was colder than anywhere else in the city, and the walls seemed to shimmer with the remnants of the Queen's power. As Lira entered the grand hall, the heat from the nearby torches did little to ward off the chill that clung to her skin. The Queen's presence was palpable, an invisible weight that hung over the room like an ever-present fog.

Queen Ysra sat upon her throne at the far end of the hall, her regal form draped in a gown made of the finest furs, the silver threads of her crown gleaming in the dim light. Her eyes, cold and calculating, locked onto Lira as she approached.

"You summoned me, Your Majesty?" Lira asked, bowing respectfully.

Ysra's gaze never wavered. "I have been hearing whispers," she said, her voice like the wind cutting through the trees. "Whispers of distractions. Whispers of rebellion. And I am not pleased."

Lira's heart skipped a beat, but she kept her composure. "I am loyal to you, Your Majesty. I have no intention of betraying that loyalty."

The Queen studied her for a long moment before speaking again. "Good. You are my most trusted guard. But I sense a shift in you, Lira. A doubt that has begun to fester within your heart. Do not let it grow. You are bound to this kingdom. To me. And to the winter we have forged."

Lira's chest tightened. She knew the Queen spoke the truth. Her heart had begun to waver, the prophecy gnawing at the edges of her thoughts. But she could not voice those fears. Not here. Not now.

"I am bound to you, Your Majesty," Lira replied, her voice steady.

The Queen seemed satisfied with her answer, but Lira could sense that Ysra was not done with her yet.

"There is something else," the Queen continued. "A visitor has arrived from the distant kingdom of Aelora. He is an envoy, sent to offer counsel on matters that concern our realm. He will be joining us for dinner tonight. You will see to his comfort. And you will ensure that he is treated with the utmost respect."

Lira's brow furrowed. An envoy? From Aelora? "What business does he have here, Your Majesty?"

Ysra's lips curled into a faint, knowing smile. "That is not for you to question, Lira. Just do your duty."

Lira bowed her head again, though her mind raced with questions. She had heard little about Aelora in recent years. The kingdom was distant, its people more myth than reality in Amara's frozen world. What could this envoy want with them?

"Of course, Your Majesty," Lira said, retreating from the Queen's presence.

As she exited the hall, the weight of the Queen's words pressed on her chest. She couldn't shake the feeling that something was about to change. Something dangerous, something forbidden. The prophecy had always seemed like a distant fantasy. But with the arrival of the envoy, with the whisper of rebellion in the air, it no longer felt so far away.

Lira's thoughts were interrupted as she exited the palace into the cold night air. The streets were eerily silent, the usual clatter of the city muted beneath the blanket of snow. As she made her way toward the dining hall, her eyes caught sight of a figure standing in the shadows, partially hidden by the tall columns that lined the entrance.

The figure stepped forward into the light, and Lira's heart skipped a beat. His features were sharp, his eyes a deep, haunting blue that seemed to burn with an intensity she had never seen before. He was tall, his dark cloak flowing behind him as though it were woven from the very night itself. And when he smiled, it was not a smile that could be easily forgotten. It was a smile that held secrets, that promised things Lira was not ready to understand.

"Lira," he said, his voice low and rich, like the sound of distant thunder. "I have been waiting for you."

His name was Eryn.

And in that moment, Lira knew that her life was about to change forever.

Lira stood frozen in place, her breath hitching as the figure before her spoke. Eryn. The name echoed in her mind like a warning bell, yet there was something compelling about him, something that tugged at the deepest part of her soul. He was unlike any man she had ever seen, his presence almost otherworldly, as though he were born from the very night that surrounded them.

For a long moment, neither spoke. Lira's hand still rested on the hilt of her sword, though she no longer felt the need to draw it. Her instincts screamed at her to remain on guard, to question his motives, but there was something in his eyes— something that made her heart flutter against her chest despite herself.

"I… I don't understand," Lira finally found her voice, though it was barely a whisper, drowned by the howling wind that cut through the streets. "You're the envoy from Aelora?"

Eryn's lips curled into a small smile, though it wasn't one of warmth. It was a smile that held secrets, mysteries she couldn't begin to unravel. "I am," he said, his voice smooth, yet laced with an edge that suggested he was not entirely who he claimed to be. "But I am also something far more than that."

Lira's pulse quickened. She knew she should turn away, return to her duties, to the path set before her by the Queen. But Eryn's gaze held her in place, as if he were the calm center of a storm, and she was being drawn to him against her will.

"What do you want from us?" she asked, her voice more steady than she felt.

Eryn stepped closer, his figure looming over her, but his presence was not menacing. Instead, it was charged with a strange energy—something ancient, powerful, and undeniably magnetic. His voice dropped, low and intimate, as if sharing a secret meant for only her.

"I want nothing but the truth," he replied. "And you, Lira, have a part to play in it."

Her heart skipped a beat, and for the first time in years, Lira felt something stir within her that wasn't cold or empty. Her pulse thrummed with a sense of urgency, a sense of destiny she could not ignore. "What truth?" she managed, her voice betraying her growing curiosity.

Eryn's smile deepened, though his eyes remained distant. "The truth about your kingdom, the truth about the curse that binds it. And perhaps most importantly, the truth about you."

A chill ran down Lira's spine. His words were heavy, as though they carried the weight of a thousand unspoken promises, and yet she understood them to be dangerous. She had been trained to guard against lies, to protect the Queen and her rule. But this man—this stranger—was different. His presence, his words, unraveled the very foundation of everything she had ever known.

"What do you mean by that?" Lira demanded, stepping back, narrowing her eyes. She could not allow herself to be swayed, not even by the strange allure that clung to him like a veil. "Who are you really?"

Eryn took another step forward, closing the distance between them. His proximity was intoxicating, as if the very air around them shifted with his movement. "I am a bearer of truths long forgotten, Lira," he said, his voice a soft, almost hypnotic cadence. "And I am here because of you. Because of what you are destined to do."

Lira swallowed, her heart pounding in her chest as his words sank into her mind. She wanted to push him away, to demand that he speak plainly, but her body refused to obey. She was tethered to him in a way she couldn't explain, drawn to the unknown pull that seemed to emanate from him.

"I don't understand," she said, shaking her head as if to clear her thoughts. "I am nothing. I am a guard. Nothing more. I have sworn my loyalty to Queen Ysra. To Amara."

Eryn's expression softened, his gaze flickering with an emotion she couldn't quite decipher. "You are more than you think, Lira. Much more. You are the key to ending the eternal winter. To breaking the curse that binds this land."

Her breath caught in her throat. The words were too much to comprehend, too impossible to accept. The curse—the one that Queen Ysra had imposed upon the kingdom with her icy reign—was not just a symbol of the Queen's power. It was a weight that held the entire world in its grip, and Lira had been raised to believe that it was a force of nature that could never be undone.

"Don't say that," she whispered, almost to herself. "The Queen… she—"

"The Queen has her secrets, Lira," Eryn interrupted, his voice sharp with a hidden urgency. "She controls the winter because it is a choice, not a curse. The eternal frost is a price she pays to keep something far darker at bay. And she has kept you in the dark about your true role in all of this."

Lira's mind raced, the words too much to process, yet they felt like pieces of a puzzle that had been scattered for years, and now, slowly, they were coming together. She had never questioned the Queen's rule, never dared to doubt the unyielding cold that surrounded her. But what if everything she had been taught was wrong?

"Why are you telling me this?" she asked, her voice trembling despite herself.

"Because you need to know," Eryn replied, his gaze never leaving hers. "Because you are the one who can end it all. You are the one who can break the curse… or keep it alive. And the choice is yours."

Lira's breath came faster now, the weight of his words crashing down upon her like the blizzard winds that swept through the city. Her thoughts were a whirlpool, pulling her deeper into a maelstrom of questions and fears. How could this man, this stranger, know such things? And why was he telling her now? Was he truly an envoy, or was there something more to his arrival? Was he the key to the very prophecy she had heard whispered in the coldest of nights?

The wind howled louder, as though the very sky was reacting

to the tension that crackled between them. For a moment, all was silent, save for the faintest echo of Eryn's words in Lira's mind. She knew what she had to do.

"Tell me everything," she demanded, her voice rising with a strength she didn't realize she had.

Eryn nodded slowly, his expression unreadable. He reached into the folds of his cloak and withdrew an ancient scroll, its edges worn and yellowed with age. He unrolled it carefully, revealing symbols that Lira had never seen before—symbols that seemed to glow faintly, as if imbued with some kind of magic that was far older than the kingdom itself.

"This," he said, "is the key to the lost magic that can break the winter's curse. It is tied to you, Lira. To your bloodline."

Lira took a step forward, her heart pounding in her chest as she gazed at the scroll. The air around them seemed to thicken, and for the first time, the frozen winds of Amara did not feel so cold. She could feel the heat building within her, the undeniable surge of something ancient and powerful stirring inside her. It was a feeling she could not explain, but one she could no longer ignore.

"Tell me what I need to do," Lira whispered, her voice barely audible, but her resolve stronger than ever.

Eryn's gaze softened, and for a fleeting moment, she saw something in his eyes—something that was not a mystery, but a promise. A promise of what could be, of what they could accomplish together.

"You must come with me," he said, his voice low and filled with conviction. "The first step of your destiny begins now."

Lira's heart raced, a mix of fear and anticipation building inside her. She knew that whatever path lay ahead, it would not be an easy one. It would be fraught with danger, with choices that could alter the course of everything she had ever known. But in that moment, standing in the frozen streets with Eryn, the choice was clear.

She nodded, her decision made. "I'll come with you."

And as they turned together, the wind howling around them, Lira felt the weight of her destiny settling upon her shoulders. She was no longer just a guard of Amara. She was the key to its salvation. Or its destruction.

Two

Frost and Fire

The night had fallen cold over Amara, its bitter chill sweeping through the stone streets of the capital. Even the palace walls, cloaked in frost, could not shield the city from the constant breath of winter that gnawed at everything it touched. Snowflakes spiraled through the air like tiny, glittering shards of ice, settling on the cobblestones in quiet layers. The moon, hidden behind a veil of clouds, cast a dull light over the city, and the wind howled like a restless spirit, sweeping through the empty alleys and winding streets with relentless force.

Lira had spent the day in the shadow of the Queen's court, her thoughts swirling with the words of the strange envoy, Eryn. Since their first meeting, something within her had shifted—something deep and unspoken, yet undeniably present. He had been nothing like she expected. His appearance alone had stirred something inside her, a spark of warmth in a place long frozen by duty and devotion to Queen Ysra. She couldn't explain it, but every moment since meeting him had left her restless, as though she were walking on the edge of a precipice, unsure whether she was about to fall or soar.

Lira's hand gripped the hilt of her sword as she made her way toward the dining hall where Eryn was waiting. It had been arranged by the Queen herself that they would meet again tonight, under the pretense of sharing a meal. But Lira knew better. This wasn't just a social occasion. There was something Eryn wanted from her—and something he was offering in return.

As she approached the great hall, the torches flared brightly, casting long shadows against the walls. The temperature seemed to drop even further as she entered the grand chamber, her boots crunching in the fresh snow that had been swept in from the outside. Her breath curled in the cold air, and the weight of her cloak felt like lead on her shoulders.

She could feel the tension hanging in the air, thick and oppressive, as if the very room was charged with a strange energy. The long table stretched out before her, covered in silver platters and crystal goblets, the faint glow of candlelight flickering from every corner. And there, at the far end of the table, sat Eryn.

He was alone, his dark cloak draped over his form like a shadow, his piercing blue eyes fixed on the fire that burned in the hearth. The flames flickered in his gaze, dancing in his irises, casting strange reflections on his face. He didn't look up as Lira entered, and for a moment, she simply watched him from the doorway.

There was something unsettling about him. Something beyond his striking appearance. His features were sharp, chiseled, almost too perfect, as though he had stepped out of a myth. But it was the air around him that drew her in—the undeniable pull, the sensation that he was not entirely of this world.

Taking a deep breath, Lira stepped forward. The crackling of the fire was the only sound in the room until the echo of her footsteps reached Eryn's ears. His eyes lifted, and for a moment, everything seemed to still.

"Lira," he said, his voice as smooth as the wind over the frozen fields. "I've been waiting for you."

His words were not cold, nor were they welcoming. They were simply there, hanging in the air between them, heavy with unspoken meaning.

Lira's throat tightened, her fingers twitching at the thought of drawing her sword. But she held herself still. She had no reason to suspect him, not yet. And besides, the mere presence of Eryn, the way he made her feel, unsettled her more than any weapon ever could.

"I wasn't sure what to expect," Lira replied, her voice betraying none of the unease swirling inside her. She had trained her whole life to be stoic, unyielding. But there was something in Eryn's presence that made her question everything she had been taught.

"You expected a man from Aelora," Eryn said, a faint smile curving his lips. "But I am much more than that."

He stood slowly, his long cloak trailing behind him like the wings of a dark bird. The firelight caught the edges of his features, illuminating the sharpness of his jaw, the lines of his face, but not quite revealing the depths of what lay beneath. His eyes—those eyes—held secrets that seemed to shimmer just beyond the reach of her understanding.

Lira crossed the room, her boots clicking softly on the stone floor. The closer she came to him, the more the temperature seemed to drop, though the fire before them burned with an unrelenting heat. It was as though the two forces—fire and ice—were locked in a delicate dance, each vying for control.

"You said that you know how to break the curse," Lira said, her voice cutting through the silence. The words felt heavy in the room, as though they were made of something much darker than mere speech.

Eryn tilted his head slightly, his expression unreadable. "Yes. I know of the magic that can undo the winter's curse. But it is not a simple thing. Magic like that is bound by ancient rules, by forces far older than any of us."

Lira's eyes narrowed. "Why are you telling me this?"

Eryn's gaze softened, but only for a moment. He stepped closer, the air around them thickening with an invisible tension. "Because you are the key, Lira," he said, his voice low, almost a whisper. "Without you, the magic cannot work."

Her heart skipped a beat. "What do you mean? I'm just a guard."

"You are more than that," Eryn replied, his voice like the crackling of the fire, his words weaving themselves into her very being. "Much more."

Lira shook her head, her mind racing to make sense of what he was saying. She had always been told that she was just one of many, a cog in the machinery of Amara. Her whole life had been defined by duty, by the cold, by the relentless winter that gripped her kingdom. There had been no room for anything else. No room for love, for warmth, for—anything that wasn't frozen solid.

But now, with Eryn standing before her, offering her

something she couldn't yet name, she felt as though everything she had known was being pulled out from under her feet.

"Why me?" she whispered, her voice breaking the silence. "Why am I the key?"

Eryn took another step toward her, his presence so powerful now that it seemed to consume the space between them. The warmth of the fire seemed to die, replaced by the unyielding chill of winter that clung to the edges of her skin.

"Because of the prophecy," he said, his voice low and steady, though there was a hint of something darker in his eyes. "The one that says love will break the eternal winter. You and I... we are bound by it. Our destinies are intertwined, Lira."

The words hit her like a thunderclap, shaking her to her core. Love. The word was foreign to her, almost laughable, given the life she had led. Her whole existence had been about survival, about loyalty to the Queen, about maintaining the balance of power in a world locked in eternal frost. Love had no place here. It couldn't.

But Eryn's eyes... they seemed to reach into her soul, pulling at something she had never felt before. There was warmth there, a warmth that burned beneath the ice. And it scared her more than anything she had ever known.

"You've known this all along, haven't you?" she asked, her voice hoarse.

Eryn didn't answer at first. Instead, he reached out, his fingers brushing lightly against her arm. The touch was soft, almost tender, and yet it sent a jolt of heat through her body. For a moment, she thought she might lose herself in it, in the warmth of his touch, the fire that seemed to burn from within him. But just as quickly, the warmth faded, replaced by a coldness that settled in her chest.

"I have known for some time," he said quietly. "But it is not just about love, Lira. It is about choice. The prophecy speaks of two souls who must reunite to break the curse. But that reunion comes at a price. And I cannot promise you that the price will be one you are willing to pay."

Lira's breath caught in her throat, the weight of his words pressing down on her like the snow that piled high against the palace walls. She had always been taught to serve, to obey, to remain loyal. But now, in the presence of this man, this mysterious figure, she felt the foundations of everything she had known begin to crack.

"What price?" she asked, her voice barely a whisper.

Eryn's gaze held hers, steady and unwavering. "The price of everything you've known. The price of the Queen's rule. The price of your own heart."

Lira stood frozen, the truth of his words settling deep within her. She could feel it—the weight of the choice she would have to make. The warmth that had begun to stir within her heart, the warmth that had been dormant for so long, now burned with a force she could not ignore.

And in that moment, she knew that nothing would ever be the same again.

Lira stood there, her heart beating loudly in her chest as the fire crackled before her, the only sound in the otherwise heavy silence. Eryn's words hung in the air between them, thick with meaning. *The price of everything you've known.* What did he mean by that? The weight of his gaze, those piercing blue eyes that seemed to look right through her, made her feel as though her very soul was laid bare for him to see.

She tried to push the feeling away, to quell the rising tide of emotions threatening to overtake her. This was not the time for weakness, for feelings she couldn't control. She had been raised to be strong, to protect Amara, to uphold the Queen's rule no matter what. But the pull she felt toward Eryn was undeniable, and it was beginning to unsettle her.

"What do you mean?" Lira's voice was steady, but her insides were a roiling mess of uncertainty. "What is this price you speak of?"

Eryn's expression softened, but only slightly. There was an intensity in his gaze that was almost painful, as if he knew that asking her to understand now would be a burden she was not yet prepared to carry.

"The curse," he said slowly, as though choosing each word with care, "was not cast on Amara by accident. The Queen did not simply choose to freeze the land for no reason. She did it to keep something far worse at bay. A force of darkness that lies beneath the ice, in the deepest caverns of the mountains. The eternal winter is the only thing that has kept it from escaping."

Lira's chest tightened. "And you believe that love can break this curse? End the winter?"

Eryn nodded, his lips pressed together in a grim line. "Yes. But the magic that can end the winter is ancient and powerful. It requires the balance of two souls, united in purpose, bound together by love. You and I, Lira, we are the ones who can do it. But…" His voice trailed off, and for a moment, he looked as though he were struggling to find the right words. "The cost is more than just a sacrifice of the heart. It will cost you everything—your loyalty to the Queen, your duty to the realm. It will mean a choice between the future of Amara and the life you've known."

Lira felt a cold shiver run through her at his words. *A choice between the future of Amara and the life you've known.* The weight of the decision settled over her like a heavy cloak, pressing down on her shoulders.

"What happens if we fail?" she asked, almost afraid to hear the answer.

"The curse will remain," Eryn said simply. "But so will the darkness beneath the ice. The Queen has kept it contained, but if the curse is not broken, it will break free. It will spread, consuming everything in its path, destroying the kingdom. And everything you've ever known will be lost. The world as you know it will be swallowed by the cold, by the shadow that grows beneath it."

Lira swallowed hard, her mind reeling. It was too much to comprehend in one moment, the enormity of what Eryn was saying. And yet, beneath the fear, there was something else—a flicker of hope, a spark of warmth that she hadn't felt in years. Was this what she had been searching for? Was this the purpose she had always been meant for? Could love truly shatter the frost that had gripped her world?

Her gaze flickered toward the fire, its flames dancing in the hearth. The warmth it provided seemed so fragile, so fleeting against the relentless cold that surrounded them. Was it even possible to break the curse, to undo centuries of frozen history? And what would it cost her to do so?

She looked back at Eryn, the intensity of his gaze pulling her in. His presence, so otherworldly, so unearthly, made everything else seem distant, as if the world outside the walls of the palace no longer mattered.

"And what of the Queen?" Lira's voice was barely a whisper, her eyes searching his face for answers she wasn't sure she was ready to hear. "What will she do when she learns that I… that we…?"

Eryn's eyes darkened, and he took a slow step forward, closing the distance between them. The air around them seemed to crackle with tension, the temperature dropping even further, though the fire blazed before them.

"The Queen will not understand," Eryn said quietly. "She will not let go of her control over Amara so easily. She will fight to keep the curse in place, to preserve her reign over the eternal winter. But the truth is, Lira, that her rule is built on lies. She has sacrificed the kingdom to keep the darkness at bay, and she has done so at the cost of your future."

Lira's breath caught in her throat. *Lies.* The word echoed in her mind like a hammer striking an anvil. She had never considered that. She had never questioned the Queen's rule, never doubted her authority. But now, standing before Eryn, the foundations of everything she had been taught were starting to crumble.

"I have served her my whole life," Lira said, her voice shaking with the weight of her thoughts. "I have been loyal to her, sworn to protect the kingdom. And now you're telling me it's all based on lies?"

Eryn reached out, his hand brushing lightly against her arm, sending a jolt of warmth through her body, a heat that seemed to push back the cold that had settled deep within her.

"Your loyalty to the Queen is not misplaced," Eryn said softly, his voice filled with an understanding that made her heart ache. "But you must see the truth. The Queen has kept the kingdom frozen, kept it in this endless winter, but in doing so, she has imprisoned her people. She has kept them from knowing the warmth, the life, that once thrived here. And now she has become a prisoner herself, bound to a curse that can never be undone unless someone chooses to break it."

Lira pulled away from his touch, the warmth leaving her skin, though it lingered in her chest, in the place where her heart beat louder now than it ever had before.

"Why me?" she asked, her voice trembling. "Why do you think I can be the one to break the curse?"

Eryn's gaze softened, and for a moment, the distance between them felt like an ocean. He stepped back, his presence seeming to grow colder as he looked down at the scroll that still rested on the table. The symbols upon it glowed faintly, as though alive with a power that Lira could not begin to understand.

"Because you are the chosen one, Lira," he said quietly. "The prophecy speaks of a soul destined to restore the balance, to reunite with the one who can end the winter. That soul… is you."

Lira's heart pounded in her chest. The truth of his words crashed over her like a wave. *Chosen.* Her mind struggled to grasp it. She had always thought of herself as ordinary, just another soldier in the Queen's guard. But now, Eryn was telling her that she was part of something much larger, something much more significant than she had ever known.

"How can I do this?" Lira whispered. "How can I—how can we—break the curse?"

Eryn took a deep breath and straightened, his eyes filled with a determination that mirrored her own growing sense of resolve.

"By embracing the truth, Lira. By embracing the love that will break the frost. But you must decide, now, if you are willing to risk everything—the Queen's wrath, your duty, your life—for the future of Amara."

The room seemed to darken as the weight of his words settled in. Lira's breath was shallow, her heart racing in her chest. The pull she felt toward him, the connection between them, was undeniable. And yet, she knew that what they were about to attempt would change everything—everything she had ever known.

Could she truly let go of everything for the chance to bring warmth back to her kingdom?

Eryn's gaze softened once more as he took another step toward her, his voice low and filled with an almost unbearable intensity.

"Time is running out, Lira. The choice is yours."

And in that moment, as the fire crackled and the cold winds howled outside, Lira knew that the path ahead would not be easy. But it was a path she could no longer deny.

Three

The Queen's Command

The air in the palace was colder than usual that morning. Even the heavy tapestries that lined the stone walls of the Queen's private chambers seemed to shimmer with a chill that pressed in on Lira like a suffocating cloak. She had been summoned, but something in the way the guards had looked at her, the way the corridors whispered with tension, told her that this was no ordinary meeting.

Lira stood before the massive double doors, their intricate carvings of ice and snow telling tales of forgotten gods, of power and sacrifices long past. The guards flanking the entrance were silent, their eyes unreadable as they stood at attention. The sound of her boots on the cold marble floor was the only thing that seemed to break the oppressive stillness.

She didn't know why, but she felt a knot tightening in her stomach. The Queen had summoned her before, but today, this felt different. The weight of her duty pressed on her shoulders, a reminder of the oath she had sworn to protect the realm. And yet, everything within her had been shifting over the last few days—the whispered words of Eryn, the truth that lay beneath the layers of her life, the undeniable attraction she felt toward him. There was no denying it anymore. Something within her had begun to crack.

With a deep breath, Lira pushed open the heavy doors.

The chamber beyond was a contrast to the coldness of the palace's outer halls. The hearth crackled with a fire so fierce it seemed to scorch the air around it. A towering figure sat at the far end of the room, her back straight, her eyes gleaming with the intensity of a storm about to break. Queen Ysra.

Lira's breath caught at the sight of her. The Queen was seated on a throne carved from ice, the shimmer of the frost casting strange patterns on her long, dark robes. Her features were sharp, her face as beautiful as it was cold, the lines of authority etched into every inch of her. She exuded power— power that was both ancient and unyielding. It was the power of the eternal winter, the very cold that ruled this land.

"Lira," the Queen's voice was like the sound of ice breaking, smooth yet chilling. "Come closer."

Lira obeyed, stepping forward into the firelight, her footsteps echoing in the otherwise silent room. The warmth from the hearth did nothing to ease the unease that was growing inside her. The Queen's gaze remained fixed on her, assessing, calculating, as if she could see every thought, every hesitation in Lira's heart.

The silence stretched, thick and uncomfortable, until Lira finally broke it. "Your Majesty," she said, bowing her head. "You summoned me."

"Indeed," Queen Ysra replied, her voice soft, yet laced with an edge. "I've been watching you, Lira. You've been… distracted."

Lira's heart skipped a beat. *Distracted?*

The Queen's eyes narrowed. "You've been… fraternizing with the envoy, haven't you?"

Lira's stomach clenched, but she held her composure, keeping her voice steady. "I have only fulfilled my duty, Your Majesty. As you commanded."

Ysra's lips curled into a thin smile, though there was no warmth in it. "Is that so?" she asked, her gaze piercing. "Then tell me, Lira, do you still feel the loyalty you once did? Or has something… clouded your judgment?"

Lira clenched her fists at her sides, feeling the weight of the Queen's words bearing down on her. She could feel the tension in the air, a palpable presence that made the temperature in the room drop even further. The flickering flames of the hearth seemed to retreat into the corners, and the walls felt even colder, as though the very room were listening for her response.

"I am loyal to you, Your Majesty," Lira said firmly, though her voice quivered despite her best efforts. "I am the Queen's guard. My duty is to protect Amara."

The Queen studied her for a moment, her expression unreadable. Then, slowly, she stood, the movement as graceful as it was menacing. Her long, dark cloak swirled around her like a shadow, and for a moment, Lira felt as though she were standing in the presence of a storm.

"Good," Ysra said, her voice a low growl. "But you must understand something, Lira. You are not just a guard. You are the protector of the eternal winter. The balance of this kingdom rests on your shoulders, and any distraction— any romantic entanglement—could destroy everything we've worked to build."

Lira's heart pounded in her chest. She knew the Queen's words were true. But what the Queen didn't understand—what she could never understand—was the fire that had been kindled inside her by Eryn. The way he made her feel alive in a world frozen by duty and sacrifice. The way he had opened her eyes to the possibility of something more.

The Queen took a step toward her, the coldness in her eyes cutting through Lira like a blade. "Do you understand what is at stake?" she asked. "You've been so focused on your duty that you've lost sight of the true cost of this kingdom's survival. The winter... the curse... they are not simply chains that bind the land. They are the price we must pay to keep the darkness away."

Lira's throat tightened. She had always known the winter was a sacrifice, a cost, but hearing it from the Queen's lips made it feel even more real, more oppressive.

"I understand, Your Majesty," Lira said, her voice barely above a whisper. "But there are... rumors. Whispers of magic, of an ancient ritual that could break the curse."

The Queen's expression darkened instantly. "Do not speak of such things," she warned, her voice cold and commanding. "That magic is forbidden. The ritual was sealed away for a reason. It is not to be touched."

Lira's mind raced, her thoughts swirling. The Queen's reaction only deepened her suspicions. If the ritual was forbidden, if it was locked away in the shadows, then perhaps it held the key to ending the eternal winter. But why was it hidden? What was the Queen truly afraid of?

"What are you hiding, Your Majesty?" Lira's words slipped out before she could stop them, and the moment they were spoken, she regretted them. She had gone too far.

The Queen's eyes narrowed, her gaze hardening into something like ice. She stepped closer to Lira, her presence towering over her.

"You think you know everything, Lira?" she asked, her voice dripping with venom. "You think you understand the weight of the choices I've made? The sacrifices I've borne? The curse that I alone carry to keep this kingdom safe from the true darkness?"

Lira swallowed hard, her throat dry. "I did not mean to offend, Your Majesty."

"You have no idea what I've given up," the Queen continued, her voice rising now, as though the words were building up inside her, desperate to escape. "The power I wield over the winter, the cold that governs this land—it is not a gift. It is a burden, a curse that I have carried for centuries. And you… you want to undo it? You want to destroy everything I've built, everything I've sacrificed?"

Lira's mind reeled. The Queen had spoken of the curse as if it were something personal, something that had cost her more than just power. But there was more to this. There was a deeper secret, something that Lira had yet to uncover. And it scared her.

"Your Majesty," Lira said, her voice trembling but firm. "I only want what is best for the kingdom. But I also want to understand. I need to know the truth. What is the real cost of the winter? What is it that you're protecting us from?"

The Queen's expression softened slightly, though there was no warmth in her eyes. "You are too young to understand the price of power, Lira. And you are too naive to see the consequences of meddling with forces you cannot control."

Lira's mind was spinning now, the weight of her internal conflict threatening to consume her. She had sworn her loyalty to the Queen. But Eryn's words, the truth he had shown her, were starting to unravel the world she had known. The Queen was hiding something, and it was becoming clear that the magic, the ancient ritual that could end the eternal winter, was not just a simple matter of breaking a curse. There was more at stake than anyone had been willing to admit.

As if sensing the storm brewing within Lira, the Queen took a step back, her gaze still locked on her. "You are dismissed, Lira," she said, her tone cold once again. "But remember this: you are not just a soldier. You are the keeper of this kingdom's future. Do not allow your heart to cloud your judgment. Do not let love—especially the dangerous kind—become your undoing."

Lira's heart pounded in her chest as she bowed, the weight of the Queen's words pressing down on her like a stone. She turned to leave, her footsteps heavy as they echoed through the cold stone halls of the palace.

Outside the Queen's chambers, Lira paused, leaning against the wall to catch her breath. The tension in her body was unbearable, the fear and uncertainty gnawing at her insides. She knew now that the Queen had secrets, secrets that would change everything. But what was she willing to sacrifice to uncover them? What was she willing to risk to find the truth?

As she stood there, torn between duty and desire, between loyalty and love, the icy winds of Amara whispered in her ears. The kingdom was on the brink of something terrible, something dark. And Lira could feel herself slipping, slipping further and further away from the path she had once sworn to follow.

The choice, it seemed, was no longer hers to make.

Not anymore.

Lira lingered by the Queen's chamber, her breath coming in shallow, controlled gasps as her mind whirled with the weight of the conversation. Every word the Queen had spoken hung in the air like a cloud of frost, chilling her to the core. *The cost of power, the burden of sacrifice*, and *the truth you are too young to understand.* The Queen had spoken of the curse and its consequences as though she alone bore the brunt of it all. But what was the truth behind her reign, and why had she hidden so much from the kingdom?

As Lira stood there, thoughts swirling in the cold silence, she heard soft footsteps approaching. She straightened, wiping her hand across her brow as if to clear the haze that clouded her vision.

It was Aric, a fellow member of the Queen's guard. He was a tall man with the same stoic demeanor as any of the Queen's soldiers, his face chiseled with determination. His presence had always offered her some comfort in the past, but now it only served to remind her of the distance between the life she had known and the uncertain future that lay ahead. Aric paused when he saw her, his sharp eyes scanning her face for any sign of distress.

"Are you well, Lira?" His voice was soft, careful, as though he could sense her turmoil. "I… I've heard about your meeting with the Queen."

Lira glanced toward him, then quickly away. "I'm fine," she lied, masking the tremor in her voice. "It's just… difficult, you know?"

Aric nodded, his expression unreadable. "I understand. The

Queen's expectations are always high. But we all serve a purpose here, don't we?"

Lira felt her heart tug at his words, the weight of her duty pressing in on her once more. She had lived her whole life with purpose—to guard, to protect, to ensure the Queen's rule never faltered. But now, with every passing moment, that purpose felt increasingly hollow, like a shell of the person she had once been.

"And what about you, Aric?" she asked, her voice quieter now. "Do you ever wonder if there's more than just this—more than just duty?"

Aric's eyes darkened slightly, but he did not answer immediately. He took a step closer, his hand resting on the hilt of his sword as if to steady himself. "The Queen's vision is clear, Lira," he said after a moment. "It's our duty to protect the kingdom, to ensure the eternal winter remains. It is our only choice. You know that as well as I do."

Lira swallowed hard, her heart heavy in her chest. She wanted to tell him—tell him everything about Eryn, about the forbidden magic, about the world beyond the walls of Amara. But the words caught in her throat, lodged there by the crushing weight of the secret she had begun to harbor.

"Yes," she murmured, though she was not entirely sure that she believed the words she spoke. "I know."

The air between them thickened, and the silence stretched until it was almost unbearable. Lira could feel Aric watching her, sensing the inner conflict that she tried to hide. She knew that he saw something in her, something that had changed, something that had shifted the course of her life forever.

"Is something bothering you, Lira?" Aric asked, his voice low, though still laced with concern. "You can talk to me. You know I'll listen."

The temptation to open up, to confide in him, was nearly overwhelming. But Lira pushed the urge away. She couldn't tell him. She couldn't risk it—not when so much was at stake. Not when her loyalty to the Queen still held her captive.

"I'm fine," Lira repeated, forcing a smile. "I just need some time to think."

Aric studied her for a moment longer, his gaze sharp, before he nodded, clearly unconvinced but unwilling to press further. "Very well. But remember, Lira, you're not alone in this. We're all part of something much larger than ourselves. The Queen depends on us, and we must never forget that."

Lira nodded, though her mind was far from the loyalty she once held for the Queen. The image of Eryn flashed in her mind—his piercing blue eyes, the warmth she felt when they were together, the way he had awakened something inside her that she couldn't ignore. He had opened her eyes to the possibility of something greater, something beyond the Queen's cold rule. And yet, the price of that knowledge was steep. The Queen had made it clear: one could not serve two masters. To embrace the truth meant to defy the Queen.

As Aric walked away, his footsteps fading down the long corridor, Lira was left alone with her thoughts. She turned slowly, her gaze falling upon the intricate, frozen windows that lined the hallway. The ice etched into the glass formed delicate patterns, frozen flowers that seemed to mock her inner turmoil. The eternal winter, she thought bitterly. It had gripped this kingdom for so long, but it was not just the land that was frozen. It was the hearts of the people, the very soul of Amara itself.

Lira's thoughts turned back to Eryn, to the forbidden magic

he had mentioned. The truth that had been hidden from her for so long. She had to know more. She had to find out what the Queen was hiding, even if it meant going against everything she had ever known.

With a resolve that burned in her chest, Lira made her decision. She would seek out the ritual. She would find the truth, no matter the cost. But how? The Queen had made it clear that such magic was forbidden, locked away in the deepest, darkest corners of the kingdom. If she was to uncover it, she would have to be careful—careful of who she trusted, careful of who might be watching.

Her first thought was Eryn. He had knowledge of the magic, of the ancient ritual that could undo the winter. But trusting him was dangerous. It was a risk, and one that could cost her everything.

She couldn't go back to the Queen. Not yet. She needed to understand what was at stake before she made her final choice. The prophecy—*the love that could break the eternal winter*—had been planted in her heart, and she felt its pull with every breath she took. But if she was to follow this path, if she was to break free from the chains of the Queen's rule, there would be no going back.

As the afternoon light began to fade, casting a shadow over the halls of the palace, Lira made her way to the library, the one place where secrets could be buried—or revealed. She had to find answers. She had to learn the truth about the ritual, about the cost of breaking the curse, and about the consequences of defying the Queen.

The library was silent as she entered, the rows of ancient books standing like sentinels in the dim light. She moved quickly, her heart pounding as she scanned the titles, her eyes searching for anything that might hold the key to the forbidden magic. Hours passed as she combed through the texts, the words blurring together, but then—there, in the farthest corner of the room, an old, leather-bound tome caught her eye.

She reached for it, the dust falling away as her fingers brushed over the worn pages. The title was faded, barely legible, but she could make out one word clearly: *Forbidden*.

With trembling hands, Lira opened the book, the ancient pages crackling beneath her touch. What she found inside would change everything.

Four

The Forbidden Touch

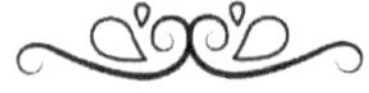

The forest outside the city of Amara was silent, save for the soft crunch of snow beneath Lira's boots as she made her way deeper into the trees. The moonlight bathed the landscape in an eerie, silvery glow, casting long shadows on the snow-covered ground. The cold was biting, the air thin and sharp in her lungs, but Lira hardly noticed. Her mind was elsewhere, pulled by something stronger than the chill that surrounded her.

She had slipped away from the palace under the cover of darkness, avoiding the prying eyes of the guards and the watchful gaze of the Queen. It wasn't the first time she had sought refuge in the forest, but tonight was different. There was something in the air, an undercurrent of anticipation, that made the decision to leave feel more urgent. She had to clear her head, to think.

But as she walked, her thoughts were consumed by a single

figure. Eryn.

His face, those piercing blue eyes that seemed to see through to the very heart of her. His touch, his voice, the way he made her feel… more alive than she had ever felt in this frozen kingdom. The pull between them was undeniable, a force that called to her like a moth to a flame. And yet, every time she thought of him, a knot twisted tighter in her chest, a mixture of longing and fear.

She could feel the weight of the Queen's words from earlier that day still heavy on her. The Queen had warned her against distraction, against love, against the very emotions that were beginning to stir within her. Love was a weakness, the Queen had said. It could destroy everything they had fought for. And yet, Lira couldn't help but wonder—what if it was love that could save them?

She stopped in the clearing, the trees surrounding her like silent sentinels, their limbs heavy with snow. The moon hung low in the sky, casting a pale light over the landscape. Lira shivered, pulling her cloak tighter around her shoulders, but it wasn't just the cold that made her heart race.

A rustle in the distance.

She turned sharply, her hand instinctively reaching for the hilt of her sword, but then she saw him—Eryn, stepping out from the shadows of the trees, his figure looming tall against the white backdrop of the snow. He was dressed in dark, flowing garments that seemed to blend with the night, his hair wild and untamed by the wind. The sight of him sent a jolt through her, and for a moment, she forgot to breathe.

"You followed me," she said, her voice barely a whisper, though she knew there was no hiding the truth in the forest. The world seemed to shrink around them, the snow falling heavier, the wind whispering secrets in the silence.

Eryn's eyes locked onto hers, his expression unreadable, but there was something in his gaze—something that felt both familiar and foreign at the same time. "I didn't follow you," he said, his voice low and steady. "I came because I knew you would come here."

Lira felt a shiver race down her spine. He was always one step ahead, always so certain, so confident. It unsettled her. And yet, there was something in his presence that calmed the storm inside her, something that made her forget the warnings of duty and loyalty that had haunted her all her life.

"What are you doing here?" Lira asked, taking a step back, her boots crunching in the snow.

"I wanted to speak with you," Eryn replied, taking a step forward. His voice was soft, but there was a thread of urgency beneath it. "You've been distant, Lira. I can feel the conflict within you. The weight of your duty, and the weight of what we both know is coming. You don't have to carry it alone."

Lira's heart beat faster as his words sank in. She could hear them echo in her mind, his promise of something beyond duty, beyond loyalty. It was a promise of something she wasn't sure she was ready to accept. The pull between them had always been there, but tonight, it felt stronger than ever. She could feel it in the air, in the way the snow had stopped falling, in the way the world seemed to hold its breath.

"I'm not… I'm not sure what you want from me," Lira whispered, her voice shaky. She didn't know why she was fighting this. The desire to give in was so strong. But every part of her screamed that it was wrong. Every part of her told her that if she gave in to this feeling, it would ruin everything. "This isn't the way, Eryn. We can't—"

"Can't what?" Eryn interrupted, his voice gentle, but there was a fire behind his words now, a fire that mirrored the heat she felt rising in her own chest. "Can't be together? Can't feel what we both know is there? Lira, this bond—it is not by chance. You and I are part of something much larger than either of us. Our connection, it is ancient. And it is the only thing that can change the world."

Lira swallowed hard, her hands trembling as she fought to control the rush of emotions that surged through her. *Ancient. The only thing that can change the world.* The words seemed to hang in the air like a trap, drawing her in deeper.

"I don't understand," she said, stepping back, her breath coming faster now. "What do you mean? What is this bond? Why is it so important?"

Eryn took another step toward her, his eyes never leaving hers, his face filled with a mixture of resolve and something else—something she could not quite place, but it was there, in the way he held himself, in the way his voice softened when he spoke her name.

"You know, Lira. Deep down, you've always known." He reached out, his fingers brushing against her cheek, sending a spark of warmth through her skin. "The prophecy. The one that has been hidden for centuries. The one that speaks of two souls destined to break the eternal winter. You and I… we are those souls. We are the key to undoing what has been done."

Lira's breath caught in her throat, the realization hitting her like a wave. The prophecy. She had heard the whispers of it, of a love that could shatter the cold, that could end the endless winter. But she had always dismissed it, thinking it nothing more than a legend, a story to pass the time on the coldest nights.

But now… now, as Eryn's touch lingered on her skin, and his words swirled around her like a spell, she could feel the weight of it. *The prophecy. The curse.* It was all real. And she, Lira, was at the center of it all.

"I didn't choose this," she whispered, her voice trembling. "I didn't choose you."

Eryn's expression softened, his hand dropping slowly to his side. "Neither did I. But some things are beyond choice, Lira. Some things are fate."

Lira looked away, her heart racing, her mind a whirlwind of conflicting emotions. The snow had begun to fall again, softly at first, but then harder, as though the world was reacting to the intensity between them. She could feel the tension between them, thick and tangible, like the storm that raged within her.

Eryn stepped closer, so close now that she could feel the heat from his body, hear the steady rhythm of his breath. The world around them seemed to blur, the trees, the snow, the night sky—all of it fading away until only the two of them remained.

"Lira," Eryn breathed, his voice barely a whisper. "You are the key to ending this curse. But the bond we share, it will not be easy. It will tear you apart if you let it."

Her pulse quickened. She could feel the warmth spreading through her body, the pull between them so strong now that she couldn't deny it. She wanted to resist, to fight it, but the yearning inside her was impossible to ignore.

"I don't know if I can do this," she whispered, her eyes closing for a moment as she tried to steady herself. "I don't know if I can give in to this."

Eryn's fingers gently cupped her chin, lifting her face to meet his gaze. The intensity in his eyes burned into her, and for a moment, Lira was lost. She couldn't think, couldn't breathe. The only thing she could do was feel.

His lips brushed against hers, soft at first, testing the waters, as if asking for permission. The moment their lips met, a spark ignited between them—wild, uncontrollable, as though the very earth beneath them trembled in response. The kiss deepened, fierce and desperate, the heat building between them like a fire that could not be quelled. Lira's hands moved to his chest, clutching at the fabric of his cloak, pulling him closer, needing more of him.

In that moment, there was no longer any room for doubt. No room for hesitation. There was only him, only the feeling of his lips on hers, of the fire that burned inside her. And yet, as the kiss deepened, a small voice whispered in the back of her mind—the warning she had pushed aside, the fear of what this moment could cost her.

When they finally pulled away, breathless and shaken, Lira's heart pounded in her chest, her body trembling with the aftershock of their kiss. She looked at Eryn, her thoughts a whirlwind of confusion and desire.

"What now?" she whispered, her voice barely audible.

Eryn's eyes were dark with emotion, his chest rising and falling with each breath. "Now we fight. For the future of Amara. For the love we share. And for the world that depends on us."

But as Lira stood there, feeling the heat of his touch still burning on her skin, she couldn't shake the nagging feeling that everything had just changed. That the path ahead—though paved with passion and desire—was fraught with danger. And the consequences of their bond might be far greater than either of them could imagine.

Lira stood in the clearing, the weight of Eryn's presence pressing in on her like the snow that surrounded them, both cold and heavy. The moonlight bathed them in its eerie glow, but all she could feel now was the heat of his touch, the fire that still simmered beneath her skin from their kiss. Her heart raced, her breath shallow as she pulled back slightly, searching his face for answers that seemed just out of reach.

The world around them was still—eerily so—save for the soft whisper of the wind stirring the trees. It was as though time itself had paused, waiting for the next move. Lira could feel the weight of everything pressing down on her. The prophecy. The Queen's warnings. The consequences of what she had just done. A single kiss had torn open a world of possibility, but it had also sealed her fate in ways she couldn't yet understand.

Eryn's hand lingered on her arm, his touch still electric, and Lira flinched, though she couldn't bring herself to pull away. She was drawn to him, an irresistible pull that she could not deny, even though everything in her screamed that it was wrong. The Queen's voice echoed in her mind—*You are the keeper of this kingdom's future. Do not allow your heart to cloud your judgment.*

But in this moment, standing beneath the moonlight with Eryn, everything felt different. The cold that had governed her life for so long seemed miles away, and she could feel warmth in her chest—a warmth that had been absent for so long it almost terrified her.

"I told you," Eryn's voice was low, his gaze intense, "we are bound by fate, Lira. This connection we share—it's not an accident. You can feel it too, can't you?"

Lira's heart pounded in her chest as she nodded, though part of her still refused to believe the reality of it. "I... I don't know what to feel. All I've known is duty, loyalty. Everything else… it seems impossible."

Eryn's lips curled into a faint smile, and there was something soft, almost sorrowful, in his expression as he stepped closer, his body mere inches from hers now. "You are not the only one who has been bound by duty, Lira. But now, it is time for us to rewrite the rules. Together."

Her pulse quickened, and the weight of his words sank in deeper. Was this truly what she wanted? What she needed? A part of her wanted to deny it, to turn away, to bury the feelings that had sprung to life between them. But another part—the deeper part—urged her to embrace it, to follow the path that had been set before her.

"You don't understand," she said, her voice thick with uncertainty. "If I—if we—pursue this, it could tear everything apart. The Queen would never allow it. She would…" Lira trailed off, the words faltering in her throat as she thought of the consequences—the Queen's wrath, the disloyalty she would be branded with. "I can't betray everything I've worked for."

Eryn's gaze softened, his hand lifting to gently cup her face. His thumb brushed against her cheek, and despite the cold, warmth spread from the point of contact, like a spark igniting a fire within her. "I don't want you to betray anything, Lira. I want you to choose what's right. You are the one who can break this curse. You are the one who can change everything. But you must decide what you're willing to fight for."

The intensity of his words hit her like a shockwave. She could feel the weight of the choice before her, the magnitude of the decision she had to make. The entire future of Amara rested on her shoulders, and yet, here she was, standing in a moonlit forest with the very man who was tied to the fate of that future. The path before her had never seemed clearer and, at the same time, more impossibly difficult.

Her breath hitched as she closed her eyes, fighting the swirl of emotions inside her. When she opened them again, Eryn was still there, watching her with an intensity that made her feel as if the world had shrunk down to just the two of them. He had seen her—truly seen her—in a way no one ever had before.

"I can't do this alone," she whispered, her voice barely audible. She didn't even know why she was saying it, but it felt true. This burden, this prophecy, it wasn't something she could carry by herself.

"You won't have to," Eryn replied softly, his voice filled with a promise that calmed the storm inside her, if only for a moment. He took another step forward, and this time, Lira didn't pull away. His face was close enough now that she could feel the warmth of his breath against her skin, the same warmth that had ignited when they kissed. "Together, we can change the world. But you have to trust me."

Lira hesitated, the knot in her chest tightening. Could she trust him? Could she trust anyone, especially now? She had sworn her life to the Queen, to the cold, to the eternal winter. To abandon that oath now would mean everything she had ever known would unravel. But the fire that burned in her chest, the connection between them that felt as if it had been written into the stars, told her that she couldn't ignore it any longer.

She took a slow, shaky breath, her hands trembling as she reached out to him. The space between them was small, but it felt like the entire world hinged on this one moment. With trembling fingers, she touched his chest, feeling the steady thrum of his heartbeat beneath the fabric of his cloak.

"I don't know what's coming," she said, her voice a whisper, "but if we do this… if we really do this… there's no turning back."

Eryn's eyes softened with understanding, and he nodded slowly, as if he had been waiting for this moment for a long time. "There is no turning back. But together, we will face whatever comes. We were always meant to do this, Lira."

Her breath caught in her throat. She wanted to believe him. She wanted to believe that what they were about to do would make the world better, that their love could truly break the curse. But deep down, she was afraid. Afraid of losing everything she had ever known. Afraid of the consequences. Afraid of what she was becoming.

"I don't know if I'm strong enough," Lira admitted, her voice barely above a whisper.

Eryn's fingers cupped her chin again, gently lifting her face so that she had no choice but to meet his gaze. His eyes were soft but intense, as though he could see every fear, every doubt, every hesitation within her.

"You are stronger than you think," he said, his voice steady and filled with an unwavering belief that she could not ignore. "You are the key to ending this, Lira. Don't let fear control you."

Lira closed her eyes for a moment, the weight of his words sinking in. The coldness of the night, the weight of the world pressing down on her—none of it mattered when she was with him. All that mattered was this moment, this choice. She could feel the warmth growing inside her, the warmth that came from knowing that, for the first time in her life, she was not alone. She wasn't just a soldier of the Queen. She was something more. She was part of something that could change the world.

When she opened her eyes again, she found Eryn's gaze locked onto hers, unwavering. Slowly, she nodded. "Okay," she whispered. "Let's do it. Let's end the curse. Together."

The moment the words left her lips, the air seemed to shift, as if the forest around them had taken a collective breath. The snowflakes fell softly around them, and the world seemed to hold its breath, waiting. Eryn smiled, the warmth in his eyes lighting up the darkness between them. His hands moved to her waist, pulling her gently toward him.

And this time, when their lips met, it was different. There was no hesitation, no fear. There was only the certainty that this was what was meant to be. The kiss was fierce, desperate, and filled with the promise of something more. Something that would change everything.

As they broke apart, their foreheads touching, breathless and shaken, Eryn whispered, "We are destined for this, Lira. This love is the flame that will end the frost. And we will burn brighter than the cold ever could."

Lira closed her eyes, letting the weight of his words settle within her. She knew, then, that there was no turning back. This bond between them was more than love—it was the key to breaking the eternal winter. And together, they would face whatever lay ahead.

Five

Secrets Beneath the Ice

The city of Amara was buried under a blanket of snow, the cold creeping through the narrow streets, curling around buildings like a living thing. It had been days since Lira and Eryn had shared their forbidden kiss in the moonlit forest, but the warmth it had sparked inside her still lingered, despite the bitter chill that defined her world. Yet, for all the fire that burned between them, she could feel the weight of what was to come pressing down on her, like an avalanche waiting to happen.

The night had grown darker as they made their way to the hidden part of the city, an area forgotten by the palace's watchful eyes. It was a place of old legends and whispers, where the ice seemed to have a life of its own, and the wind carried secrets of long-buried truths. As they walked through the abandoned streets, the buildings around them had been swallowed by the snow, only their silhouettes visible in the faint glow of the lanterns.

"Are you sure this is the place?" Lira asked, her voice barely audible over the wind's howling. She glanced at Eryn, whose face remained impassive, his eyes scanning the darkness ahead of them.

"Trust me," Eryn replied, his voice calm, though there was an edge to it that made Lira's heart race. "The temple is here. I know it. I've felt it for years."

Lira's heart skipped a beat at the certainty in his voice. He had told her little about the temple, only that it was hidden beneath the city, buried under layers of snow and ice, and that it held the key to the magic that could break the curse. The closer they got to the place, the more Lira felt a strange unease settle in her chest, as though the very air around them was thick with the weight of centuries.

They turned down a narrow alley, the buildings around them seeming to close in like a maze, and stopped before a seemingly ordinary stone wall. Lira looked at it, her brow furrowing. There was nothing remarkable about it—just another wall, covered in layers of frost and snow, the jagged ice reaching up toward the sky.

Eryn stepped forward, his fingers brushing against the surface of the wall, and for a moment, nothing happened. Then, with a faint hum of magic, the stone began to shift. The ice that had built up over the years cracked, revealing a hidden doorway, its frame lined with ancient runes that glowed faintly in the dim light.

Lira gasped, stepping back in surprise. She had heard of magic like this—ancient, forbidden magic—but to see it unfold before her eyes was something else entirely.

Eryn's gaze softened as he turned to her. "Are you ready?"

Lira's pulse quickened. She nodded, though she wasn't entirely sure what she was stepping into. Her mind still raced with the choices before her—the Queen's rule, the love she felt for Eryn, and the weight of the prophecy that seemed to bind them together. But one thing was clear: this was the path she had to take, whether she was ready for it or not.

"After you," she said, her voice steady despite the turmoil inside her.

With a single, fluid motion, Eryn pushed the door open, revealing a dark passageway that seemed to stretch endlessly beneath the city. The air was colder here, sharper, the very walls slick with ice. Lira shivered, but her curiosity drove her forward, following Eryn down the winding path.

The tunnel was narrow, the walls closing in as they descended deeper into the earth. The further they went, the more Lira felt the weight of history pressing down on her, as though the very stones were alive with the secrets of the past. The air grew heavier, and the sound of their footsteps echoed in the silence, amplifying the tension between them.

After what felt like hours, they reached a large chamber, its size surprising after the narrow, winding passage they had traversed. The room was vast, the walls adorned with ancient carvings of ice and stone, depicting scenes of battles long forgotten, gods and creatures of legend. The floor was covered in a thick layer of frost, and in the center of the room stood an altar, its surface covered in more runes, glowing faintly with a light that seemed to pulse in time with Lira's heartbeat.

Eryn stepped forward, his gaze never leaving the altar. "This is it. The heart of the magic."

Lira followed him, her breath shallow as she took in the sight. The air in the room was thick with power, ancient and unyielding. It felt as though the very temple itself was holding its breath, waiting for something to happen.

"What do we do now?" Lira asked, her voice barely a whisper.

Eryn turned to her, his eyes locked onto hers with an intensity that made her heart skip a beat. "We need to unlock the magic," he said quietly. "And to do that, we have to activate the bond between us. It's tied to the prophecy. The magic will only respond if we—"

He didn't finish his sentence, because at that moment, a sound broke the silence. It was low, almost imperceptible, like a soft whisper carried on the wind. But it was enough to make Lira's heart race. She turned toward the entrance of the chamber, her senses suddenly alert, her hand instinctively moving to the hilt of her sword.

The sound grew louder, a low rumble that seemed to come from deep within the earth. The walls of the chamber began to shake, the ancient carvings on the walls seeming to twist and writhe as though they were alive. The light from the altar flickered, casting strange shadows across the room.

Eryn's eyes widened. "It's starting. We have to act quickly."

Before Lira could respond, the ground beneath them cracked with a deafening noise. The stone floor split open, sending shards of ice and rock flying into the air. A gust of cold air shot up from the fissure, and the room was filled with the sound of something ancient and powerful stirring beneath them.

Lira stumbled back, her hand reaching out to steady herself. Eryn was already moving, his body tense with purpose as he approached the altar. The glow from the runes intensified, and for a moment, Lira thought she saw a figure standing in the shadows—an ancient being, cloaked in shadow and ice.

She blinked, and the figure was gone.

"The magic is awakening," Eryn said, his voice strained. "We need to activate the bond now, before it's too late."

Lira's heart pounded in her chest, her mind racing. She had no idea what was happening, but she knew one thing for sure—this was no ordinary magic. Whatever was hidden beneath the city, whatever ancient force was awakening, it was tied to her, tied to the bond she shared with Eryn.

With trembling hands, she stepped forward, her gaze never leaving Eryn's. The intensity in his eyes matched the power of the magic that was swelling in the room, filling the space with a force she could almost taste.

"You need to touch the altar," Eryn said, his voice urgent. "Together. Our bond will trigger the magic."

Lira swallowed hard. The air around them seemed to grow colder, the temperature dropping so rapidly she could see her breath in front of her. The ground trembled beneath their feet, and the sound of the earth splitting grew louder. She could feel the tension building, the pressure of the moment making it hard to breathe.

She took a step toward him, her feet heavy, her body unwilling to move, as though the weight of the choice had rooted her to the spot.

Eryn's hand reached out, and without thinking, Lira took it. The instant their hands met, a surge of energy shot through her, filling her veins with an intensity that was both painful and exhilarating. The room around them seemed to pulse with life, the air thick with power.

Together, they approached the altar, the runes glowing brighter, the magic intensifying. Lira's breath hitched as she felt the connection between them deepening. Their souls seemed to reach out to each other, intertwining in a bond that was both beautiful and terrifying.

As their hands touched the cold stone of the altar, a flood of images and sensations filled Lira's mind. She saw the past—the curse, the ancient magic that had bound the kingdom in ice, and the sacrifice that had been made to keep the darkness at bay. She saw herself, standing at the center of it all, her love for Eryn the key to ending the eternal winter.

But as the magic surged through her, something dark stirred beneath the surface. A voice echoed in her mind—a warning.

The cost is greater than you know, Lira. The magic will break the curse, but at what price?

Lira's heart raced as the altar shook beneath her hands, the power surging through her, threatening to consume her. She could feel the weight of the decision pressing down on her, the knowledge that the world she knew would be torn apart if they succeeded.

But the bond between them was undeniable. It was the key.

With a final, desperate breath, Lira closed her eyes, surrendering herself to the magic, knowing that there was no turning back.

The room exploded with light.

And the world trembled.

As the light faded, Lira stood there, gasping for breath, her hands still resting on the altar. The chamber was silent once more, the magic now pulsing quietly in the air, like a heartbeat.

Eryn stood beside her, his hand still gripping hers. His face was pale, his expression unreadable. The air was still, but the weight of what they had done hung in the balance.

Lira's heart thundered in her chest. "Did it work?" she asked, her voice barely a whisper.

Eryn didn't answer immediately. Instead, he looked down

at the altar, his face shadowed with uncertainty. Then, slowly, he turned to her, his eyes filled with both awe and fear.

"It's begun," he said quietly. "But we don't know what the cost will be."

The room felt colder now, as though the magic had left an icy trace in its wake. And Lira knew, deep down, that this was only the beginning of what was to come.

Lira's heart thudded in her chest as the last remnants of the magic flickered and dimmed, leaving the chamber in an eerie silence. The air was thick with a charged energy, heavy with the aftereffects of what they had just triggered. Her hands still trembled as she slowly pulled them away from the altar, the cold stone still humming faintly beneath her fingertips.

Eryn stood motionless beside her, his eyes dark with something Lira couldn't quite place—fear, maybe, or the realization of what they had just set in motion. She felt a cold breath on her neck and turned to him, searching for any answers in his gaze.

"What does this mean?" Lira asked, her voice barely above a whisper, the weight of the moment pressing down on her like the snow that buried the city above them. "Did we break it? The curse?"

Eryn's jaw tightened as he stepped back, his eyes still fixed on the altar, his brows furrowed in deep thought. He didn't seem to hear her question right away, as though he was still processing everything that had just occurred. The runes on the altar had dimmed, but their glow still lingered in the air, like ghosts of the magic that had surged through the room. The energy that had filled the space was now slowly dissipating, leaving behind only an unsettling stillness.

"No," he finally said, his voice quiet but firm. "The curse is not broken—not yet. But something has shifted. We've awakened the magic, Lira. We've triggered the process."

Lira's pulse quickened as she looked around the chamber, her eyes scanning the walls, the intricate carvings, and the ruins of forgotten power. The room felt colder now, a stark contrast to the heat that had burned through them only moments ago. A cold, suffocating weight settled around her, and for a brief moment, she wondered if they had made a terrible mistake.

"I don't understand," she murmured, taking a step back from the altar. "You said the bond between us would trigger the magic. Why does it feel like… we've just unleashed something worse?"

Eryn's face was etched with concern, but there was something else there—something deeper. Guilt, perhaps? Or regret?

"The magic is more than just a tool to break the curse," Eryn said, his voice barely a whisper now. "It's a force. It is tied to the very essence of the land. The balance of winter. The forces of nature that keep the kingdom in its frozen grip."

Lira's stomach twisted as she processed his words. "So, we've done more than just awaken the magic. We've disturbed it, haven't we?"

Eryn didn't answer at first. His gaze shifted to the walls of the chamber, and for a brief moment, Lira thought she saw the flicker of something dark in his eyes—something ancient, buried deep beneath the surface.

"There is something… dark beneath all of this," Eryn said, his voice growing distant, almost lost in thought. "The magic is tied to the curse, yes, but it is also tied to something else— something much older. A force that was sealed away to protect the kingdom, to keep the worst of it from breaking free. The ritual we've just completed… it has weakened the seal."

Lira's breath hitched, her heart racing in her chest. "You mean to say… that there's something even darker than the curse? Something we've just… unleashed?"

Eryn nodded slowly, the weight of his words sinking in like a heavy stone. "Yes. The curse was never the true enemy. It was just the barrier keeping something far worse at bay. A darkness that, if allowed to return, could swallow everything we know. The curse, the winter… it was the only way to keep it contained."

Lira felt her legs grow weak beneath her as the full implications of Eryn's words crashed down on her. The cold, the frost, the endless winter—it was never meant to be a punishment, but a protective measure. They had unlocked something that could destroy everything, not just the world of ice, but the world itself.

Her throat tightened as she glanced back at Eryn, his face pale, his eyes filled with the weight of the choice they had just made. "What now?" she whispered. "What do we do now?"

Eryn's expression softened, and for a moment, Lira saw the conflict in his eyes. The man who had been so confident, so sure of the path they were on, now seemed uncertain—torn between what they had unleashed and what they had hoped to achieve.

"We have to undo it," he said, his voice resolute but tinged with a weariness that didn't sit well with her. "We have to re-seal the magic, Lira, before it's too late. Before the darkness breaks free."

A sense of panic surged through her, and she stumbled back, her eyes searching the walls for some clue, some way out of the nightmare they had stumbled into. "But how?" she asked, her voice cracking. "How do we undo it? How do we stop this?"

Eryn looked at her, his expression full of sorrow and determination. "We need to return to the altar. The bond we formed—our love—it is the key. But there is one more step we must take."

Lira felt a tremor ripple through her body. She had heard the stories of the prophecy, of the love that would break the curse, but never had she imagined it would lead to something like this. The force they had awakened… It was something beyond her comprehension, something that had been locked away for a reason. And now, the burden of it all weighed heavily on her—heavier than the cold that had always defined her life.

Eryn stepped toward her, his hand reaching out to gently touch her arm. The warmth of his skin against hers was a stark contrast to the chill that had settled in the air. For a moment, their eyes met, and the world around them seemed to fall away. There was no Queen. No kingdom. No curse. Only them, and the bond they shared.

"We can do this," he said, his voice low and steady. "But we must be willing to sacrifice everything. Your loyalty to the Queen, the kingdom itself… everything."

Lira closed her eyes, the weight of his words pressing down on her chest. The Queen had warned her about love—the dangers of distraction, of defying duty. And yet, standing here, in the heart of the temple, with Eryn by her side, she realized that everything she had known had been a lie. The Queen, the kingdom, the cold—it was all built on a foundation of fear, of sacrifice.

"I don't want to lose this," she whispered, her voice filled with the uncertainty of what lay ahead. "I don't want to lose you."

Eryn's face softened as he stepped closer, his forehead resting against hers. "You won't. But to save everything… we must make the choice. We must give everything."

The words hung in the air between them, heavy and inevitable, and Lira felt the full force of what they meant. The magic was not just the key to ending the eternal winter—it was the key to their very survival. But using it came with a cost—a cost that she could not yet fully understand.

The ground beneath them shifted, a low rumble echoing through the chamber, and the walls of the temple began to glow with an unnatural light. The air around them crackled with power, and Lira knew, with a terrible certainty, that they were running out of time.

"Lira," Eryn's voice broke through her thoughts, pulling her back to the moment. "We have to make the choice now."

Her heart pounded in her chest, the weight of the decision pressing on her shoulders. She had lived her life for duty, for the Queen, for a kingdom that had been locked in ice for centuries. But now, with Eryn standing before her, she saw the truth. The curse, the Queen, the ice—it was all a lie. The real danger lay beneath them, waiting to break free.

She turned toward him, her eyes meeting his with a fierce determination. "Then let's do it. Let's end this."

The altar pulsed with light, and the runes on the walls glowed brighter. They had made their choice. Together, they would face whatever came next. And in that moment, as the magic surged around them, Lira knew that the world would never be the same.

The Frostbite of Betrayal

The cold wind howled through the city, whipping the snow into frenzied swirls that seemed to echo the storm inside Lira's chest. She could hear the crunch of footsteps behind her, too steady, too familiar. When she glanced over her shoulder, she saw Aric, his tall figure outlined against the pale city walls, his brow furrowed in concern. He had been following her for a while now, ever since the night in the temple, and Lira could feel the weight of his gaze as it bore into her back.

She hadn't meant to betray him, to keep the secret of her growing relationship with Eryn. But now, she felt as if her very heart were exposed to the freezing winds of the world. Aric had always been her closest friend, someone she trusted implicitly, but now, everything was different. Her betrayal wasn't just about Eryn—it was about everything she had ever known, everything she had sworn to uphold. The Queen's guard, her duty to the Queen, the vows she had made—all of it was beginning to feel like a distant memory, like it belonged to someone else.

"Lira," Aric called out, his voice sharp, cutting through the howling wind. "I need to speak with you."

She stopped, her feet sinking slightly into the snow as she turned to face him. The expression on Aric's face was a mixture of confusion and something darker—something that chilled her to the core. His eyes narrowed, his jaw set in a hard line. He was no longer the trusted comrade she had known. Now, he was a stranger, a reflection of what she had done.

"What is it?" Lira asked, her voice tight, betraying none of the chaos swirling inside her.

Aric stepped closer, his boots crunching loudly in the snow, the sound like thunder in the stillness. "I know what's been going on, Lira. I know about you and him."

Lira's stomach twisted, her breath catching in her throat. The words felt like a slap, though she had known this moment was coming. She had hoped, for just a moment, that she could keep the truth hidden, that no one would find out, but she had been wrong. Aric knew.

"You don't know what you're talking about," she said quickly, her voice betraying the panic rising in her chest. She couldn't explain to him, not like this. Not in the middle of the street where anyone could overhear.

"Oh, I know," Aric shot back, his voice low, filled with the sharp edge of betrayal. "I know about your meetings, about the way you look at him. You've been meeting him in secret, haven't you?"

Lira swallowed hard, her mind racing for the right words, but there were no words that could undo what had already been done. How could she explain to Aric that her feelings for Eryn were not a betrayal, but a force she could not resist? How could she tell him that the love she had for the man from Aelora was tied to something far bigger than either of them, that it was a bond that might save—or destroy—the world?

"I didn't mean for this to happen," Lira said, her voice trembling. "But I—I can't change it, Aric."

A flash of something darker crossed Aric's face. The hurt in his eyes was palpable, but there was something else there too. Anger. And perhaps something deeper—disappointment.

"I never thought you'd betray me like this," Aric said, his voice tight. "I've always had your back. And now, you're helping him, the very man who could destroy everything the Queen has worked for. Everything we've fought for."

Lira recoiled at his words, but they cut through her, each one landing like a blow. She opened her mouth to respond, to explain, but the words wouldn't come. There was no easy explanation for what she had done. And worse, she wasn't sure that there was a way to go back.

"I'm not betraying anyone," Lira said finally, her voice steadier now, though her heart was pounding in her chest. "You don't understand, Aric. You don't know what's at stake."

"Oh, I understand all right," Aric spat, his eyes flashing with anger. "The Queen has given everything for this kingdom. And you—" he shook his head, disgust creeping into his voice "—you're willing to throw it all away for a man. A man you barely even know."

"I know him better than you think," Lira said, her voice low and sharp, her words laced with a conviction she didn't fully understand herself. "And this isn't about him. This is about the future of Amara. This is about breaking the curse. The

Queen's rule… it's not what you think it is."

Aric's eyes narrowed, his jaw clenching. "The Queen's rule is absolute. She has protected us from the darkness. And you, you're willing to risk everything for a dream? For a prophecy? You've lost your way, Lira."

A sickening twist of guilt gnawed at Lira's insides, but she held her ground, refusing to let the weight of Aric's words break her. She had made her choice. She had seen the truth in Eryn's eyes, felt the bond between them, and she couldn't turn away from it. Not now. Not when the fate of everything she knew depended on it.

"Aric," Lira said softly, her voice steady now despite the chaos inside her. "I don't want to hurt you. But I can't keep pretending. I can't keep living in a lie."

Aric stepped back, his hands balling into fists at his sides. His chest rose and fell with the force of his breath, his face twisted in a mix of pain and rage.

"I've had enough of this, Lira," he said, his voice hard and cold. "You've made your choice. Just know that this—this thing with him—it's going to cost you. You'll lose everything. The Queen will never forgive you."

Before Lira could respond, Aric turned sharply and stormed off into the snow, his silhouette quickly swallowed by the swirling white. She stood there, rooted to the spot, the weight of his words hanging heavily in the air, pressing down on her chest.

But before she could gather herself, the sound of approaching footsteps broke through the silence again. This time, the steps were slower, deliberate. Lira knew exactly who it was before she even turned to face the newcomer.

A chill ran down her spine as Queen Ysra's imposing figure

appeared at the edge of the alley, her silhouette framed by the snowstorm. Her cloak shimmered in the light of the street lanterns, the frost clinging to her like an extension of her power. Her eyes, cold and calculating, locked onto Lira with a gaze that was both familiar and terrifying.

Lira's breath caught in her throat as the Queen approached, her every step deliberate, echoing through the stillness of the city. Lira had always known this moment would come—the moment when the Queen would discover her defiance. But facing it now, in the biting cold, with Aric's betrayal still fresh in her mind, left her feeling more exposed than ever.

"Lira," the Queen's voice rang out, icy and unforgiving. "I need to speak with you."

Lira nodded, though her throat tightened with fear. She knew what was coming. The Queen's cold eyes narrowed as she stopped a few feet away, her presence looming like the storm itself. There was no warmth in her gaze, no trace of the affection Lira had once imagined might exist between them.

"I know," the Queen said, her voice smooth, controlled. "I know about you and Eryn."

Lira's heart skipped a beat. She swallowed hard, her thoughts racing. "I… I didn't mean for it to get out. It was—"

"No need for explanations," the Queen cut her off, her voice laced with authority. "I've seen enough. You've been meeting him in secret, haven't you? Disrupting the balance, betraying your oath."

Lira's stomach twisted. "I'm not betraying anyone, Your Majesty," she said, trying to steady her voice. "I—I'm only trying to help."

"You are helping no one," the Queen snapped. "You're putting everything at risk. The very fabric of this kingdom is at stake, Lira, and you've chosen to side with someone who seeks to undo everything I've sacrificed."

The Queen's words were like daggers, each one cutting deeper than the last. Lira stood silent, her chest tightening as the weight of her actions bore down on her.

"You've broken your oath," the Queen continued, her voice growing colder, sharper. "And now, you will face the consequences."

Lira's heart pounded in her chest as she stepped forward, her hands trembling. She had never thought it would come to this—the Queen, her mentor, her ruler, standing before her, accusing her of treachery. But Lira knew, deep down, that this moment was inevitable.

"I'm sorry," Lira whispered, her voice barely audible. "But I cannot go back. Not after everything I've learned."

The Queen's gaze turned icy, and for the first time, Lira saw something flicker behind those cold eyes—something dark, something dangerous.

"You are a fool," the Queen said quietly, her tone filled with finality. "But I am not without mercy. You will be given a chance to prove your loyalty. If you fail…"

Lira's blood ran cold at the threat hanging in the air. The Queen's voice dropped to a dangerous whisper. "If you fail, you will lose everything. Your life. Your love. And your kingdom."

With those words, the Queen turned on her heel, her cloak swirling behind her as she disappeared into the snowstorm, leaving Lira standing in the cold, her heart heavy with the knowledge of what was coming next.

Lira stood frozen in the snow, her heart hammering in her chest as the Queen's figure vanished into the storm. The wind howled around her, but it felt like nothing compared to the storm raging within her. Her legs felt weak, as though the very ground beneath her was giving way. The Queen's words, laced with both finality and threat, echoed in her mind. *You will lose everything. Your life. Your love. Your kingdom.*

The weight of it all was suffocating.

Her thoughts spiraled, tumbling over themselves. She couldn't go back. Not after everything she had learned, everything she had felt. The Queen had been right about one thing: the bond between her and Eryn was no longer just a passing infatuation—it was a force, a truth that had woven itself into the very fabric of her being. But the choice was never supposed to be this difficult. She had never imagined that her loyalty to the Queen would be tested this way. She had always been taught that duty came first, that the kingdom and its people were more important than her own desires.

But now, she felt torn. Eryn had shown her a different path, a path that led to breaking the eternal winter, a path that could free Amara from the icy grip that had held it for centuries. And yet, standing here in the heart of the city, knowing that Aric had betrayed her and that the Queen was watching her every move, Lira felt as though the walls of her world were closing in.

Suddenly, a voice broke through her thoughts, low and hesitant.

"Lira?"

She turned sharply to find Aric standing a few paces away, his face strained with the same mixture of hurt and anger she had seen before. His posture was tense, his shoulders tight with suppressed emotion, but there was something else—something deeper in his eyes. He was no longer the friend who had always been by her side, the one who had fought alongside her for the Queen. No, now he was a stranger, someone who had seen her betrayal, someone who felt the sting of her defiance.

"What are you doing here?" she asked, her voice hoarse, though she didn't really want to know. She already knew the answer.

"I should ask you the same thing," Aric replied, his voice cold, but tinged with something—disappointment? Pain? "I never thought you'd betray everything we've fought for. For him."

Lira winced at his words, though they cut deeper than she cared to admit. "You don't understand, Aric. This isn't about him. This is about breaking the curse. About saving the kingdom."

"And you think *he* can do that?" Aric's voice broke with disbelief. "You think *he*—someone from a foreign kingdom, someone whose very presence threatens our queen—can save Amara?" He shook his head, eyes blazing. "You're blinded by him, Lira. The Queen—she's given everything for us. She has sacrificed *so much*, and you—"

"I *know* what the Queen has done," Lira snapped, cutting him off. Her heart pounded in her chest as the words spilled out, raw and unfiltered. "But what if everything she's done is a lie, Aric? What if the winter isn't a curse, but a choice? What if there's something *worse* hidden beneath all this?" Her chest tightened as she spoke, the weight of the truth pressing down on her. "You don't understand…"

"You're wrong," Aric said, his voice low and dangerous. He took a step toward her, his eyes hard. "And I don't care what he's told you. The Queen's rule is the only thing that keeps Amara from falling into chaos. If you keep going down this path, you're going to tear this kingdom apart."

Lira's breath caught in her throat as his words hit their mark. The guilt she had tried to push aside crept back, lacing its way through her thoughts. *What if Aric was right? What if she was risking everything for a man who had already shown her the power of their bond, but hadn't revealed the full extent of what it could cost?*

But the truth clawed its way back to the surface—the truth of the temple, the magic they had unlocked, the knowledge that the Queen's rule had never been as clear-cut as it seemed. And in the deepest part of her, Lira knew that she could never ignore the truth that Eryn had awakened in her. She couldn't deny it, no matter how hard she tried.

"Aric…" She took a deep breath, her eyes searching his face for something—anything—to hold onto. "I don't know what's going to happen next. I don't know if I'm making the right choice. But I can't stand by and watch Amara remain in the ice forever. There's more to this curse than we've been told. And I can't pretend it doesn't matter."

Aric was silent for a long moment, his face dark with conflict. His eyes softened, though, just for a second, before they hardened again. "I never wanted to fight you, Lira. But I can't let you do this. The Queen will never forgive you. And neither will I."

Lira's chest tightened at the finality in his voice, but she didn't flinch. She couldn't. "Then you have to decide, Aric," she said quietly. "I've made my choice."

Before he could respond, a distant voice interrupted them, rising from the shadows of the street. "Lira?"

Both Lira and Aric turned at the sound of her name, and Lira's breath hitched in her throat. The figure emerging from the darkness was familiar—too familiar—and her heart skipped a beat at the sight of him.

It was Eryn.

His face was partially obscured by the shadows, but there was no mistaking the intensity in his eyes. His gaze flicked between Lira and Aric, the tension thick between them.

"Eryn," Lira whispered, her pulse quickening. She wanted to step toward him, to close the distance between them, but the storm of emotion inside her held her in place.

"What is this?" Aric demanded, his voice rising with a mixture of confusion and anger. "Are you part of this? Are you the one who's been leading Lira astray?"

Eryn's jaw tightened, and he stepped forward, his eyes locked on Aric. "I'm not here to fight with you," he said, his voice calm but firm. "I'm here because I'm the only one who knows what needs to be done. What Lira needs to understand. This isn't just about love. This is about saving Amara."

"Don't try to manipulate her," Aric snarled, taking a step forward, his body tense with fury. "She doesn't belong to you."

Lira's heart twisted at the words, her chest tight as she glanced between Aric and Eryn. This was it—the breaking point. The fracture between everything she had known and the unknown future she was stepping into.

"I've made my decision," Lira said, her voice steady despite the storm of emotions raging inside her. "And I need to do what's right for Amara. For all of us."

Aric's eyes hardened, but he didn't speak. Instead, he turned away, storming off into the snow. His back was stiff, his gait heavy with finality. Lira watched him go, feeling the distance between them grow with each step he took.

A cold silence settled between her and Eryn. The moment felt like an eternity, and Lira could feel the weight of her actions pressing on her chest, suffocating her. The truth was undeniable, and yet, so was the sacrifice.

Eryn finally broke the silence, his voice low and filled with a sense of urgency. "Lira, we don't have much time. The Queen will make her move soon. We need to act."

Lira nodded slowly, the weight of the moment sinking in. The Queen's shadow loomed larger now, and she knew that nothing would be the same from this point forward. What had started as a whisper in her heart had grown into a full-fledged storm, and there was no turning back.

She looked at Eryn, her heart still unsure, but resolute. "I'm ready," she whispered.

The storm around them seemed to quiet as they turned toward the future—toward the battle that would determine the fate of Amara. But deep inside, Lira knew that no matter what happened next, she had already crossed a point of no return. And there would be no coming back from the choices they had made.

The weight of betrayal had already set its roots deep within her, and the consequences were only just beginning.

Seven

Heart of Ice

The moon hung heavy over Amara, casting its pale light over the city like a silent observer of the growing unrest within its walls. The wind howled through the frozen streets, a reminder of the icy grip the Queen held on her kingdom. Yet beneath the cold, beneath the fortress of ice that surrounded the palace, there was something else—a growing tremor, a whisper of rebellion that echoed in the hearts of the people.

Lira stood on the balcony of her chambers, her gaze cast out over the city. The familiar sights—the white-tipped rooftops, the snow-covered streets—now seemed foreign to her, as though the world she had known her entire life was slipping away. The wind tugged at her cloak, pulling her deeper into the embrace of the night.

She could feel the tension in the air, like the calm before a storm. The Queen's grip on the realm was tightening, but it was no longer as secure as it once was. The rumors of dissent, of unrest, were growing louder. The people of Amara were beginning to question the endless winter, and the Queen's hold over them was slipping. They were beginning to stir, to push back against the icy tyranny that had ruled them for centuries.

Her thoughts were interrupted by the sound of footsteps behind her. She didn't need to turn to know who it was. Eryn. The pull between them, the bond that had formed in the temple, was still as strong as ever. And yet, despite the warmth that had blossomed between them, there was a chasm growing inside her—a chasm she couldn't ignore. The Queen. Her loyalty to the Queen. The kingdom. Everything Lira had known her whole life. It was all coming undone.

Eryn stopped beside her, his presence a steady force in the otherwise cold night. The wind tugged at his cloak, but he stood unmoving, his eyes fixed on the distant horizon, as if searching for something beyond the city walls.

"You've been quiet lately," Eryn said, his voice low, though the urgency in it was unmistakable. "What's on your mind?"

Lira didn't answer immediately. Instead, she stared at the city below, her thoughts swirling in a mix of confusion and dread. She had already made her choice, hadn't she? Her heart knew it, but her mind still clung to the loyalty she had been raised with.

"I don't know anymore," she said finally, her voice barely above a whisper. "Everything is so… tangled. I feel like I'm standing at the edge of a cliff, and if I take one more step, everything will crumble beneath me."

Eryn's gaze softened as he stepped closer to her, his hand brushing hers, the warmth of his touch grounding her in the chaos. "You're not alone in this, Lira. I'm with you, always."

Lira turned her face toward him, meeting his eyes. The intensity in his gaze made her breath catch. He wasn't just any man. He was the last of a forgotten bloodline, the one who held the key to ending the eternal winter. And yet, it wasn't just the magic that pulled her to him. It was the truth in his words, the promise of something greater than the world she had known. But could she really leave it all behind? Could she abandon her oath, her duty to the Queen, for a love that could either save or destroy them all?

"I know," she said, her voice thick with emotion. "But what are we really doing, Eryn? What is it you want from me? What's the real cost of breaking the curse? I can feel it, but I don't understand it."

Eryn's expression darkened, and he stepped back slightly, as though gathering his thoughts before speaking. When he spoke again, his voice was grave, heavy with something he had been holding back.

"I am the last of a forgotten bloodline," Eryn began, his eyes meeting hers with a quiet intensity. "The bloodline that was meant to break the curse, to restore balance to Amara. But to do that, we must destroy the source of the Queen's power. The relic that she controls—the one that binds the winter to this land. It is hidden in the heart of the frozen mountains."

Lira's heart skipped a beat at his words, the weight of them pressing down on her like a hundred stones. "The relic," she repeated, the word feeling foreign on her tongue. "You want to destroy it?"

Eryn nodded slowly, his gaze unwavering. "Yes. But it is not as simple as it sounds. The relic is tied to the Queen's magic. Without it, the curse will break. The winter will end. But at a cost. The Queen's power, her control over the land, is bound to that relic. If we destroy it, we destroy her. And with her… the kingdom will be left vulnerable."

Lira's breath caught in her throat. "You're asking me to choose between my loyalty to the Queen and everything I've ever known, and the future of this kingdom?"

Eryn's gaze softened, his eyes filled with a mixture of sorrow and hope. "I'm asking you to choose what's right. The Queen's rule has kept the kingdom in perpetual winter, but it has also trapped the people. Her sacrifice has come at a terrible price. The darkness that she has kept at bay is waking, and it will consume everything unless we break the curse."

Lira's heart was a battleground. She had always been loyal to the Queen, had always believed that her reign was the only thing keeping Amara safe. But now, the truth seemed so much more complicated. Eryn had shown her the world beyond the Queen's walls—the world where love and freedom could exist, where warmth could return to a kingdom frozen by fear and tyranny. And yet, destroying the Queen would mean the end of everything Lira had ever known.

"I don't know what to do," she whispered, her voice breaking. "If I follow you, I risk everything. The Queen's wrath, the wrath of the kingdom, and even my own heart. I don't know if I can live with that."

Eryn stepped closer, his hand gently resting on her shoulder, grounding her in the moment. "I'm not asking you to abandon everything, Lira. I'm asking you to help me change it. Together, we can end the winter. Together, we can give the people a future, free from fear, free from the cold that has ruled them for centuries. But it will only work if we trust each other. If we trust the bond we share."

The weight of his words settled over her like a thick blanket, heavy and suffocating. She had never felt so torn, so divided between two worlds. The loyalty she had to the Queen, to the life she had known, seemed to pull her back, while the love and hope Eryn had awakened in her urged her forward.

She closed her eyes, the sound of her breath the only thing she could hear now, her thoughts spinning like the wind outside. The decision was impossible, and yet, she knew deep down that there was no turning back. If she continued on the path with Eryn, she would lose everything she had built her life on. But if she stayed with the Queen, if she upheld the old order, she would be condemning herself—and the kingdom— to a life of eternal winter.

Lira's hands clenched at her sides, the cold bite of the night air reminding her of the world around her. She could feel the pull of her past, the Queen's icy rule that had shaped her every thought, every decision. But she could also feel the warmth of Eryn's presence, the love that had grown between them despite the chaos, despite the dangers.

Her heart ached with the weight of the choice, but she knew what she had to do.

"I will go with you," Lira said, her voice steady despite the storm raging inside her. "I will help you destroy the relic. But not because of love. Not because of you. I'm doing this for Amara. For the people who have suffered under the Queen's rule. For the future."

Eryn's eyes softened, and a small smile tugged at the corner of his lips. "Thank you," he said, his voice filled with gratitude. "You won't regret this, Lira. Together, we can make a difference."

Lira nodded, her heart still heavy with doubt, but the certainty of her decision settling within her. The path ahead was fraught with danger, but there was no turning back now. She had chosen her future. They had chosen it together.

"Let's go," she said, her voice firm now, the resolve in her heart burning brighter than ever.

With a final glance at the city that had once been her home, Lira turned away, Eryn beside her. The road ahead was uncertain, and the stakes had never been higher. But the flame that burned within her was stronger than the frost that had ruled her world for so long. And she was ready to face whatever came next.

Together.

The journey into the heart of the frozen mountains was unlike any that Lira had ever known. The air grew thinner with each step, the cold more biting, until the very wind itself seemed to claw at their skin. The snow beneath their feet was deep, treacherous, and the path ahead felt endless, as though the mountains themselves were trying to stop them from reaching their destination.

Lira and Eryn traveled in silence for the most part, the tension between them palpable. Lira could feel the weight of her decision with every step, a constant reminder that she had left the life she knew behind—everything she had ever believed in, everything she had fought for. The Queen's voice still echoed in her mind, sharp and unforgiving. *You will lose everything.*

The thought sent a chill through her, colder than the wind that whipped around them. But she didn't look back. Not anymore.

Their path wound deeper into the mountains, the jagged peaks towering above them like ancient sentinels. The further they went, the more oppressive the atmosphere became. The trees thinned, giving way to rock and ice, the sky above an unbroken sheet of gray, as though the world itself had forgotten the warmth of the sun. Lira pulled her cloak tighter around her, trying to block out the biting cold that seemed to seep into her bones. But even the physical discomfort could not outweigh the tension she felt in her chest, the gnawing uncertainty of the choice she had made.

Eryn's presence beside her was a strange comfort, though it also heightened her sense of dissonance. His calm demeanor, the unwavering certainty in his eyes, only made her feel more torn. She had chosen to follow him, to help him destroy the relic that held the Queen's power, but what would it truly mean? Would this decision free the people of Amara from the curse of winter, or would it leave the kingdom vulnerable, exposed to even greater dangers?

Every step they took seemed to take them further from the world she had known. The cold grew more suffocating, and the sound of their footsteps was the only thing that broke the silence. For hours, they trudged through the snow-covered landscape, the mountains rising like an impenetrable wall around them. The air grew thinner, colder, until Lira's breath was shallow, her body aching from the long journey.

Finally, after what felt like an eternity, they reached a clearing, a vast, desolate plateau that stretched out before them. The wind howled through the space, sending snowflakes swirling in chaotic patterns. In the distance, Lira could just make out the silhouette of an ancient structure, its outlines barely visible against the backdrop of the mountains.

"This is it," Eryn said, his voice low and filled with awe.

Lira followed his gaze, her heart pounding in her chest as

she took in the sight of the ruined structure. It was a temple, ancient and weathered by time, its stone walls cracked and worn by centuries of neglect. The very air around it seemed to hum with power, the remnants of magic that had long since been sealed away.

"What is this place?" Lira asked, her voice hoarse, a mixture of wonder and fear in her heart.

"This is the heart of the Queen's power," Eryn replied, his eyes never leaving the temple. "This is where the relic is hidden. And it is where we must destroy it."

Lira's heart skipped a beat. The temple stood like a tomb, its walls silent witnesses to the centuries of secrets buried within. The weight of what they were about to do hung heavily in the air, and she could feel the pressure building within her chest. This was it—the moment that would change everything. The moment that would decide the fate of Amara.

Eryn stepped forward, his eyes locked on the temple. "Are you ready?" he asked quietly, his voice carrying a note of both resolve and uncertainty.

Lira hesitated for a moment, her mind racing with conflicting thoughts. She had come this far, but could she truly go through with it? Could she destroy the very thing that had given the Queen her power, the very thing that had kept the kingdom in a frozen stasis for centuries? And yet, could she continue to follow a path that was leading Amara to the brink of destruction?

"I don't know," Lira whispered, her voice barely audible in the wind. "But I know I can't go back."

Eryn turned to her then, his gaze steady and unwavering. "We do this together," he said softly, his hand brushing against hers. "Whatever happens, we face it together."

The warmth of his touch was like a spark in the cold, and for a moment, Lira allowed herself to feel it—allowed herself to feel the connection between them, the bond that had been formed in the depths of the temple. But the weight of their task was never far from her mind.

They approached the temple, the stones underfoot cracked and weathered, as though the very earth had grown tired of holding them. The doors of the temple loomed before them, ancient and imposing, covered in thick layers of frost. Eryn stepped forward and placed his hand against the door, his fingers glowing faintly with the magic that had already begun to awaken. With a low rumble, the doors slowly creaked open, revealing the darkness within.

Lira's breath caught in her throat as she stepped into the temple. The air inside was cold—colder than anything she had ever felt before—and the walls were covered in runes that pulsed with an eerie, otherworldly energy. It felt as though the very stone itself was alive, watching them, waiting for them to make their move.

Eryn led the way, his movements sure and confident, though Lira could sense the underlying tension in him. He was walking into a place that held not just the relic, but also the last remnants of his bloodline's legacy. He had told her that his family had been tasked with breaking the curse, and that the relic was the key. But as they moved deeper into the heart of the temple, Lira couldn't help but feel a sense of foreboding. The relic was not just a tool—it was a part of the kingdom itself, a part of the Queen's power. Destroying it might very well destroy everything they knew.

The path grew narrower as they descended deeper into the temple, the air growing colder still. The walls closed in around them, the runes on the stone glowing brighter, their light casting strange, shifting shadows across the walls. At the end of the hallway, Lira could see a faint glow, a shimmering light that seemed to pulse with a dark energy.

"That's it," Eryn whispered, his voice tight. "The relic."

Lira's heart raced as they approached the glowing object. It was a stone, ancient and carved with symbols that were almost unrecognizable. It sat atop a pedestal, surrounded by a ring of ice that seemed to radiate with power. The air hummed with the intensity of it, and Lira could feel the pull of the relic, its magic drawing her closer.

Eryn stepped forward, his expression set with determination. "This is it. The source of the Queen's power."

Lira's throat tightened as she looked at the relic. It was beautiful, in a way, though the beauty was tinged with danger. The stone seemed to shimmer in the dim light, its energy almost palpable in the air.

"What happens when we destroy it?" Lira asked, her voice trembling with a mix of fear and uncertainty. "What will happen to Amara?"

Eryn turned to her, his eyes filled with a sorrowful understanding. "It will be free, Lira. But so will the Queen's power. She will no longer be able to control the curse. And the kingdom… the kingdom will be vulnerable. Without the winter, without her rule, there will be chaos."

Lira's heart dropped at the thought. She had never imagined that destroying the Queen's power would have such consequences. The Queen had always been the constant, the unyielding force that held everything together, even if it was in a frozen, oppressive way. Without her, what would become of Amara?

But the answer was clear: they had to act. They had no choice. The winter had to end. The darkness that had been hidden beneath it had to be kept at bay.

"I'm ready," Lira said, her voice steady despite the fear in her chest. "Let's do it."

Eryn nodded, stepping forward to place his hands on the relic. The light around it pulsed, growing brighter, and for a moment, Lira thought she could hear the whispers of ancient voices in the air. Eryn closed his eyes, focusing on the magic, the bond they shared.

And then, with a final, decisive movement, Eryn shattered the relic.

The explosion of energy was immediate. The air cracked with the force of the magic, and the ground beneath them trembled. The temple seemed to groan, as though the very foundation of Amara was being torn apart. Ice shattered, stone cracked, and a blinding light filled the room, blinding Lira for a moment.

When the light finally dimmed, Lira blinked, disoriented. The air around her felt different—warmer, though not by much. The magic had been released, but at what cost? She felt a strange emptiness inside her, a sense of loss she couldn't quite understand. The air was still cold, but there was something else now—a new tension, a new uncertainty.

Eryn stood before her, his face pale, his body trembling slightly from the exertion of the magic. "It's done," he said, his voice hoarse.

Lira didn't answer immediately. She was still processing the enormity of what they had just done. The relic was destroyed, the Queen's power shattered, and Amara was free. But the price of that freedom was yet to be seen. The consequences of their actions would unfold in the days to come.

"We've done it," Lira said quietly, her voice filled with a strange mix of triumph and dread. But as she looked at Eryn, she knew that their journey was far from over. The path ahead was uncertain, and the true cost of their decision was still unknown.

Eight

Ice In The Heart

The wind howled through the mountain pass, a bitter scream that cut through the silence of the night like a blade. It was an unnatural cold, a bite so deep it seemed to burrow into Lira's bones. The ground beneath her feet was packed with snow so thick it felt like she was walking on a layer of glass, each step careful and deliberate. Above her, the jagged peaks of the frozen mountains loomed like towering sentinels, their dark outlines against the pale sky hinting at the ancient power they held within.

Lira's breath came in shallow, visible gasps, the cold seeping into her lungs with each exhale. Her cloak whipped around her, flapping violently in the wind, but still, she didn't stop. She couldn't. Not when everything she had ever known was at stake.

Beside her, Eryn moved with a quiet determination, his stride unbroken by the treacherous landscape. His presence was a constant anchor in the storm of thoughts that raged within her. His figure, tall and resolute, contrasted with her own sense of confusion, of being torn in a thousand directions. The closer they got to the heart of the mountains, the more she felt the weight of the decision she had to make pressing down on her.

Eryn was the last of a forgotten bloodline, a bloodline that carried the ancient magic that could end the curse of eternal winter. He had already shown her the power of their connection, the bond that had awakened in the depths of the temple beneath Amara, but that bond, that magic, could cost them everything.

They had been walking for hours, the cold and the silence between them growing thicker with every step. Lira had tried to push away the doubts that crept into her mind, the doubts that told her she was making a terrible mistake. She had always believed in duty, in the Queen, in the unyielding ice that had defined her life. But now… now she wasn't so sure.

Her loyalty to the Queen had been absolute, forged through years of training, of sacrifice, of service. The Queen had been the ruler of Amara, the one who had kept the kingdom safe from the chaos that could have consumed it. But what if the Queen's grip had never been about protection? What if it had been about control? What if the Queen had never been the savior she claimed to be, but the architect of Amara's suffering?

Lira couldn't ignore the gnawing suspicion anymore. She couldn't ignore the truth that Eryn had shown her—the truth of a magic that had been sealed away, the truth of a darkness that had been hidden beneath the ice. If what Eryn said was true, then the Queen's rule had been based on a lie. But could she really be the one to end it all? Could she destroy the very power that had held the kingdom together, that had kept the darkness at bay?

Eryn's voice cut through her swirling thoughts. "We're close now," he said, his tone low and steady. "The relic is hidden in the heart of the mountains, deep within a temple that has been untouched for centuries. The Queen's power is bound to it."

Lira glanced up at him, her throat tight. She had always known that the Queen's power came from somewhere, but she had never imagined it was tied to something as ancient as this. "The relic," she repeated, her voice barely a whisper. "The source of her power."

"Yes," Eryn said, his voice edged with the weight of what they were about to do. "To break the curse, we must destroy it. But doing so will tear down everything the Queen has built. The ice, the winter, her rule—it will all come crashing down."

Lira's heart pounded in her chest. She had known this moment was coming, but now that it was here, it felt like the ground was shifting beneath her feet. Eryn had told her the truth, shown her the reality of what the Queen's reign had cost them, and yet… she still couldn't shake the fear that clung to her like a shadow.

"If we destroy it," she said, her voice shaking despite her best efforts, "what will happen to Amara? To the people? Without the Queen's power, what's left?"

Eryn stopped in his tracks, turning to face her. The intensity in his eyes was almost too much to bear, but there was a softness there too, a tenderness that she had never seen before. He reached out, his hand brushing hers, and for a moment, the cold of the mountains seemed to fade, replaced by the warmth of his touch.

"It's not about the Queen's power, Lira," Eryn said, his voice quiet but resolute. "It's about freedom. The curse, the winter—it's not just the Queen's doing. It's a consequence of the magic she controls. When we destroy the relic, we break the cycle. We free Amara from the chains of ice. But we must act now. If we wait, the power of the relic will slip away from us, and the darkness will rise."

Lira stared at him, her heart a whirlwind of emotions. Freedom. But what kind of freedom? A kingdom with no ruler, no protector? The Queen had ruled with an iron fist, but she had kept them safe. Or so Lira had always believed.

But now, everything was different. The truth had been laid bare before her. The Queen's grip was not just on the kingdom—it was on the people themselves. And if they destroyed the relic, they destroyed the Queen's hold on the realm.

Eryn stepped closer, his presence pulling her in like a force of nature. "This is your choice too, Lira. You're not alone in this. We do this together."

Lira felt a lump form in her throat as she looked up at him. The trust in his eyes, the hope, the love—it was overwhelming. He had chosen her, chosen to place the fate of Amara in her hands, and for the first time in her life, she knew that she had a choice. Not just for herself, but for the people, for the future of Amara.

"I can't go back," she whispered, the words slipping from her lips before she even realized she had spoken them aloud. "I can't go back to a life of lies. Not now."

Eryn smiled softly, a warmth in his eyes that melted the last of her hesitation. "Then we go forward," he said. "We face what comes next together."

They continued their journey, the temple looming ahead

like a dark promise, its shadow stretching over the land. The path grew steeper, the snow deeper, but Lira felt the pull of the temple growing stronger with every step. The air was thick with magic, ancient and powerful, and as they drew closer, she could almost feel the relic calling to them, beckoning them toward it.

The wind howled louder, the storm intensifying as they reached the foot of the temple. The structure itself was half buried in snow and ice, the stone walls covered in thick layers of frost. Ancient symbols carved into the stone seemed to glow faintly in the dim light, pulsing with a power that made the hair on the back of Lira's neck stand on end.

"This is it," Eryn said quietly, his breath visible in the cold air. He reached for her hand, and this time, Lira didn't hesitate. She grasped his hand tightly, her pulse racing as they stepped forward, into the heart of the temple.

The temperature inside the temple was even colder, the walls lined with ice that shimmered like glass. It was as if the very essence of the winter itself had been woven into the stone. They moved silently, their footsteps muffled by the thick layers of snow that covered the floor.

The deeper they went, the more oppressive the air became. The walls seemed to close in around them, and the weight of the magic pressed down on Lira's chest, making it hard to breathe. She could feel the relic ahead, pulsing with energy, calling to her, but she didn't know what would happen once they reached it.

Finally, they reached the heart of the temple, a large chamber that seemed to pulse with power. In the center of the room stood a pedestal, and atop it, the relic—an ancient stone, carved with symbols that seemed to glow with an otherworldly light.

Lira felt a shiver run down her spine as she approached it. The power of the relic was overwhelming, and for a moment, she hesitated. Could they truly destroy it? Could she really sever the Queen's hold on Amara?

Eryn stepped forward, his eyes locked on the relic. "This is it," he said, his voice steady but filled with an underlying tension. "We destroy it, and the curse ends. The winter ends. But we cannot turn back."

Lira looked at him, her heart in her throat. She could feel the weight of the decision pressing down on her, but there was no turning back now. The future of Amara was in their hands.

With a final, deep breath, Lira nodded. "Let's do it."

Eryn moved forward, and together, they reached out for the relic. As their hands touched the stone, a surge of energy shot through the room, a blinding light filling the temple. The walls cracked, the floor trembled beneath them, and Lira felt the magic surge through her like a wave, crashing over her, drowning her in power.

And then, as the light began to fade, the sound of a voice—low, cold, and commanding—filled the chamber.

"You think you can destroy everything I've built?"

Lira's heart stopped. The voice was unmistakable.

It was the Queen.

Before them, the air shimmered, and the figure of Queen Ysra appeared, her eyes blazing with fury, her cloak swirling around her like a tempest. The temple seemed to tremble beneath her presence, and the walls shook with the force of her power.

"You cannot escape the consequences of your actions," the Queen said, her voice icy and filled with malice. "You have made your choice, Lira. But the price will be higher than you can imagine."

Lira's heart pounded in her chest, but she stood her ground. This was it. The final battle for Amara's future.

And she was ready to fight.

The Queen's presence filled the chamber with an oppressive weight, her form emerging from the shadows like an ancient storm, her eyes glowing with fury. The cold seemed to intensify, the air thickening with a raw, almost unbearable magic. Every inch of the temple vibrated with the force of her power, and Lira could feel it deep in her chest, a heavy pressure that threatened to crush her.

Eryn stepped forward, his stance solid, his eyes unwavering as he met the Queen's gaze. He had warned her—he had told her the Queen would come, that the relic's destruction would awaken something darker than they had anticipated. But standing here, in the very heart of the temple, with the Queen before them, Lira couldn't help but feel small. The power in this room was beyond her comprehension, ancient and unyielding.

"You think you can destroy everything I've built?" the Queen repeated, her voice cold and laced with venom. "You think you can just undo centuries of sacrifice, of control? You are fools, both of you."

The words stung, cutting through Lira like a blade, but they didn't break her. She had chosen this path, and now she would face the consequences.

"We don't have a choice," Lira said, her voice steady despite the tremor that ran through her. "Your rule has kept this kingdom in a prison of ice for centuries. The people are suffering. They deserve a future."

The Queen's eyes narrowed, her lips curling into a twisted smile. "And what future will they have, Lira? A world without balance, without order? Chaos would consume them. You've broken the bond that held the kingdom together. And for what? A fleeting hope that will shatter just as quickly as the winter you tried to erase."

Lira's heart clenched, but she didn't look away. "I'm not erasing the winter, Your Majesty. I'm ending the curse. The curse that traps the people in fear. The curse that binds them to your power."

The Queen's expression darkened, her features hardening with a fury that seemed to freeze the very air around them. "You think I am the cause of the curse?" she asked, her voice growing colder, more dangerous. "You are naïve. The curse was never about me, or about control. It was a sacrifice. A choice I made to protect this kingdom from something far worse."

Lira's breath hitched at her words, and for a moment, she felt the ground shift beneath her feet. The Queen's gaze was unwavering, the intensity of her stare unyielding as she continued.

"The curse was never meant to be a punishment," the Queen said, her voice almost a whisper now, but the power behind it made every word feel like a hammer striking Lira's chest. "It was a protection. A barrier to keep an ancient evil at bay. And now, you've done the one thing that will destroy everything I've sacrificed for. You've freed the darkness."

Lira took a step back, her mind racing. "What are you talking about?" she demanded, confusion flooding her thoughts. "What darkness?"

The Queen's lips trembled with barely contained rage, and

for a brief moment, the room seemed to darken further. The light from the shattered relic flickered and dimmed as if the very magic of the temple was fighting against what they had done.

"You've heard the whispers, haven't you?" the Queen said, her voice now thick with a dangerous undertone. "The stories of an ancient power, one that predates even the winter. A darkness so ancient, so powerful, that it was sealed away for the survival of the realm."

Eryn moved slightly, his gaze still locked on the Queen, but Lira could feel the tension rising between them. The air was thick with impending conflict, and Lira could hear the echoes of the magic in the temple, like a distant rumble before a storm.

"The winter," the Queen continued, her eyes glinting with something between anger and desperation, "was never the curse. It was the price I paid to hold back what lies beneath. The relic you destroyed—its magic binds the winter, but it also keeps the true darkness sealed away. When you shattered it, you broke the seal. And now, it's coming."

The words hung in the air like a storm cloud ready to burst. Lira felt the weight of the truth in the Queen's voice, but a part of her refused to believe it. The Queen had always been the ruler, the keeper of Amara's fate. She had never spoken of the darkness, never mentioned the true cost of her power. And now, Lira was supposed to accept that she had unwittingly set loose something more dangerous than the winter?

Lira shook her head, trying to push back the fear that threatened to consume her. "No. You've manipulated us all. The curse, the winter—it's your doing. You've used it to control us, to keep us under your thumb."

The Queen's expression hardened, her jaw clenching as she

glared at Lira. "You think I wanted this? Do you think I chose to be bound to this cursed power? No. I sacrificed everything to protect this kingdom. I gave up my humanity, my freedom, to keep that darkness from consuming us all. But now, you've freed it."

The room trembled again, the magic of the temple fighting to stay contained. Lira could feel it, the oppressive weight of the unseen force pressing down on her chest, suffocating her. The cold that had once been a constant companion now felt like a living thing, an icy presence that was growing stronger by the second.

"What is it?" Lira whispered, her voice breaking. "What's the darkness? What are you really protecting us from?"

The Queen's gaze flicked to Eryn, then back to Lira, her expression hardening further. "It's not what you think. This isn't about power. It's about survival. The darkness that lies beneath is not of this world. It's a force of pure destruction, a being that feeds on fear, on pain, on the very essence of life itself. I sealed it away with the power of the relic, but you've shattered it, and now it's free."

Lira's breath caught in her throat. A force of pure destruction? The weight of the Queen's words crashed down on her, and for the first time since they had begun this journey, Lira felt the full enormity of their actions. They hadn't just broken the Queen's power—they had set loose an ancient evil, one that could destroy everything.

Eryn stepped forward, his eyes filled with determination. "Then we have to stop it. We have to find a way to seal it away again."

The Queen's expression flickered with something between disbelief and fear. "You think you can just *seal it away* again?

After everything you've done? There is no magic left to contain it. The darkness is free. And so is the price of your rebellion."

Lira's heart pounded in her chest, the terror building with every word the Queen spoke. They had thought they were freeing Amara from the curse, from the endless winter. But instead, they had opened the gates to something far worse. Something that could wipe out everything they had fought for.

"What happens now?" Lira asked, her voice barely above a whisper. "What are we supposed to do?"

The Queen looked at her with cold, steely eyes. "You want to save Amara? You have no choice now. You must face the darkness. It will come for you, for all of us, and if you fail, nothing will remain. Not even the winter."

Lira's thoughts raced, but they were interrupted by a low, menacing growl—a sound that seemed to come from deep within the earth itself. The ground beneath them trembled again, and this time, Lira could feel it—an ominous presence, a shifting darkness that seemed to pulse with malevolent intent.

The Queen's face paled, and for the first time, Lira saw something like fear in her eyes. "It's here," the Queen whispered. "Too late. The darkness is here."

The air grew colder, colder than it had ever been, and the very walls of the temple seemed to pulse with an unnatural force. Lira turned to Eryn, her heart racing as the truth settled in. The relic was destroyed, and with it, the barrier that had kept the darkness at bay.

It was coming.

And there was nothing they could do to stop it.

Nine

The Weight of the Frost

The mountains loomed ahead, their jagged peaks like the teeth of a great beast, biting at the sky. The winds howled across the snow-laden expanse, whipping the landscape into a frozen frenzy. The world before Lira and Eryn was a wasteland of ice and stone, a place where life had no place, where only the bitter cold and the endless frost ruled. The journey ahead of them was long, perilous, and filled with the kind of danger that could end them both. But there was no turning back. Not now.

Lira's breath came in short, visible bursts as she trudged through the deep snow, her legs aching with each step. The wind sliced through her cloak, the cold biting into her skin. It wasn't just the weather that made her feel exposed; it was the feeling that they were being hunted—that every step they took brought them closer to the Queen's reach. Every move they made was dangerous. They were rebels, traitors, and now fugitives, forced to flee from the only home Lira had ever known.

She glanced at Eryn, his tall frame cutting through the snow-drifts with purpose. His face was grim, his brow furrowed as he scanned the horizon, ever alert. His movements were fluid, his focus sharp, but she could see the toll this journey was taking on him as well. Their bond, the one that had been forged in the heart of the temple, had only grown stronger since the destruction of the relic. But with that strength came the burden of knowing that the Queen's soldiers were not far behind them, hunting them relentlessly.

Lira swallowed hard, trying to suppress the fear that crept into her chest. They had already encountered a few scouting parties from the Queen's forces, each one easily avoided, but each encounter had made the weight of their mission more real, more suffocating. The Queen's wrath was like a shadow following them, threatening to swallow them whole.

"We have to keep moving," Eryn's voice cut through the wind, his words carrying a hint of urgency.

Lira nodded, forcing herself to push through the cold. The frozen wilderness stretched endlessly before them, the snow and ice offering little in terms of shelter. The only sounds were the howling wind and the crunch of their footsteps, the silence pressing in on them like an unspoken truth.

"The temple," she said, her voice barely above a whisper, "how much further?"

Eryn's eyes remained fixed on the horizon, but she could see the flicker of something—determination, perhaps—pass through his expression. "It's not far. We'll make it by nightfall."

Lira didn't respond, though her heart ached with the weight of his words. They had no choice but to reach the temple. It was the only place that might hold the answers they needed to stop the Queen's growing power—and perhaps even the darkness she had unleashed. The temple was said to be ancient, buried beneath the ice, hidden away for centuries. But if it was the key to their survival, to Amara's survival, then it was their only hope.

They pushed on, the miles seemingly stretching into infinity, each step dragging them deeper into the wilderness. The wind had picked up again, fierce and biting, as though the world itself was trying to keep them from reaching their goal. The terrain grew more treacherous, the snow thickening with every passing moment, until it felt like they were wading through a sea of frozen water. Lira's legs burned with exhaustion, the cold seeping into her bones.

And yet, she didn't stop. Not for a second. Not when she could feel Eryn's presence beside her, steady and unwavering. They were in this together—this journey, this fight—and there was no turning back.

Hours passed, and the sun began to dip low in the sky, casting the landscape in a strange, dim light. The snow began to fall in thick, heavy flakes, blotting out the last of the daylight, until all they could see was an endless sheet of white. Lira pulled her cloak tighter around her, her breath visible in the freezing air. Her fingers were numb, her face windburned and raw, but she kept her eyes fixed on Eryn's back, the steady rhythm of his movements pushing her forward.

It wasn't until the wind died down that Lira allowed herself to slow. The air was still, the world around them suffocatingly quiet. Eryn had come to a halt, his body tense, his senses alert.

"What is it?" Lira asked, her voice strained.

Eryn's eyes darted around the landscape, his hand instinctively going to the hilt of his sword. "We're being followed."

Lira's pulse quickened. Her head snapped around, scanning the darkening horizon, but she saw nothing. Just the endless expanse of white, the silent wilderness stretching out before them.

"Are you sure?" she asked, her voice low, trying to keep the panic from creeping into her chest.

Eryn nodded, his jaw tight. "I can feel it. We've been tracked. Someone's been watching us."

The realization hit Lira like a punch to the gut. The Queen's soldiers were closing in. They couldn't afford to stay in the open. Not now, not when they were so close to the temple.

"Can we outrun them?" she asked, her voice urgent, her mind racing.

Eryn didn't hesitate. "Not if we stay here. We need to find shelter. Now."

Without another word, he turned, his feet already carving a path through the snow. Lira followed him, her heart pounding in her chest, adrenaline pushing her forward. They moved quickly, dodging the treacherous snowdrifts and keeping an eye out for any signs of their pursuers. The further they ventured, the deeper the night grew, and the more desperate Lira felt. She could hear the sound of the wind again, but this time, it wasn't just the wind. There were voices, muffled by the storm, but unmistakable.

The soldiers were closing in.

Eryn stopped abruptly, and Lira nearly ran into him. He raised his hand, signaling for silence. The sounds around them shifted, and Lira froze, straining her ears to catch the faintest movement.

In the distance, she saw the shadows of figures moving

swiftly through the snow. Their faces obscured by cloaks, their movements precise and coordinated. They were getting closer.

"They're almost here," Eryn muttered, his voice low and tight. "We can't fight them off in the open. We have to find a place to hide."

Lira's mind raced as they scrambled for cover. The snow and ice offered little in terms of shelter, but just ahead, she spotted a cave—its entrance barely visible beneath a mound of snow and rock. Without hesitation, they rushed toward it, the sound of their footsteps muffled by the thick snow.

Once inside, they crouched in the dark, the cold of the stone walls biting into their skin as they pressed themselves into the shadows. The cave was small, barely enough room for the two of them, but it would have to do. Eryn's breath came in shallow gasps, his body tensed and ready to spring into action at a moment's notice.

Lira's chest heaved with exertion, her heart racing, but she didn't speak. Not yet. The soldiers were close, but she could still hear nothing. She held her breath, praying that the shadows would protect them.

Minutes passed. Each one felt like an eternity.

Then, she heard them.

The crunch of boots in the snow, the sound of voices growing louder as they neared the cave's entrance. Her heart thudded in her chest, and she looked at Eryn, her eyes wide with fear. They couldn't stay here much longer. Not with the soldiers just outside.

Eryn's hand closed around hers, squeezing gently in reassurance, but there was no time for comfort. They had to act.

The soldiers passed by, their movements quick and deliberate. Lira held her breath, the world narrowing to the sound of her own heartbeat. She could feel the cold seep deeper into her bones, the dampness of the cave creeping into her skin, but she didn't move. Not even a breath.

The last soldier's footsteps faded, and Lira finally exhaled, the tension in her body slowly unwinding. They were safe—for now.

Eryn stood first, his body a dark silhouette in the dim light. "We move at first light," he whispered, his voice firm. "We can't stay here long."

Lira nodded silently, her mind still racing with the weight of their escape. The Queen's soldiers had been too close, and there would be more coming. The temple wasn't far, but they still had to survive the night.

As they settled into an uneasy rest, Lira couldn't shake the feeling that they were being watched. The night felt too still, too quiet. Outside, the wind howled, but here in the dark, it was as if the whole world was holding its breath.

As her eyes closed, exhaustion pulling her under, the weight of what lay ahead seemed to settle on her shoulders once again. They were so close, and yet, so far.

Tomorrow, they would face the temple—and whatever truths it held.

But tonight, they survived. And in this frozen wilderness, that was all that mattered. For now.

And yet, as sleep claimed her, the echoes of the Queen's words seemed to haunt her. *The storm of rebellion is gathering strength.*

Lira didn't know how much longer they could keep running.

The cave was cold, but the silence was worse. Lira lay awake long after the shadows of sleep began to creep in, the chilling air seeping through her cloak and into her bones. Every faint rustle outside, every gust of wind, every creak of the earth felt amplified, and her senses were heightened to their breaking point. She could hear the soft sound of Eryn's breathing beside her, steady but uneven, the only comfort in a world that felt suddenly foreign and full of peril.

The soldiers had passed, but the danger still loomed. They were moving deeper into the wilderness, closer to the heart of the frozen mountains, but now there was more than the Queen's soldiers hunting them. There was the weight of their decisions, the knowledge that they had released something far darker than they had ever imagined.

Lira turned her head slightly to glance at Eryn, his silhouette barely visible in the dim light that filtered through the entrance of the cave. His face was shadowed, his eyes closed, but there was an unmistakable tension in his features. He had been through this before—this feeling of running, of being hunted, of knowing that every step taken could be their last. And yet, he never showed it. Not outwardly.

She envied that. But more than that, she trusted him.

"Eryn?" Her voice was barely a whisper, but in the silence of the cave, it felt loud.

His eyes flickered open instantly, the blue of his gaze like ice reflecting the pale moonlight. "Are you alright?" His voice was rough, a little strained, but it was full of concern.

Lira didn't know how to answer that question. *Am I alright?* she thought, her chest tight with the weight of everything that had happened, of everything that was still to come. But the truth was, she wasn't sure what being "alright" even meant anymore.

"No," she admitted softly. "I keep thinking about what the Queen said… about the darkness that's been released. We've broken something, Eryn. And I don't know if we can fix it."

Eryn shifted closer to her, the motion smooth and deliberate as he sat up slightly, his hand reaching for hers in the dark. His touch was a lifeline, something warm and real in the midst of the frozen world around them.

"We didn't break it, Lira," he said quietly. "We only exposed it. It was always there, waiting. But now that we know what's at stake, we can fight it. We can stop it. Together."

The comfort of his words was fleeting, like a light that barely pierced the darkness surrounding them. But still, Lira clung to it. Together. They had always been stronger when they were together.

"But what if we're not enough?" she asked, her voice breaking just a little. "What if we can't stop it? The Queen… She said it would consume everything."

Eryn's hand tightened around hers, his voice fierce but calm. "Then we fight until there's nothing left of us but the choice we made. We fight because we *can* stop it. We have to believe that, Lira."

Her pulse quickened at his words, the sincerity in his voice igniting something deep inside her. She had always believed that the Queen's rule was absolute, that there was nothing that could break the cycle of winter. But now, in the heart of this frozen wasteland, she wondered if they might be able to rewrite the rules—if they could be the ones to undo the destruction that had bound the kingdom for so long.

"Are you ready for this?" she asked, her voice softer now, the weight of the question settling between them. The path ahead was unclear, and though they had come so far, the hardest part still lay ahead.

Eryn hesitated only for a moment before answering. "I am. Because I'm not alone."

Her heart swelled at the simplicity of his words. The bond they shared, forged through danger, through sacrifice, through the breaking of old boundaries, was something that had brought them this far. And now, as they faced the temple, as they stepped into the unknown, it was all they had to hold on to. The love, the trust—they were their only hope.

Lira nodded slowly, though her mind still raced with doubt. "Then let's finish this," she whispered.

Eryn smiled faintly, but there was no humor in it. Just the quiet acceptance of the reality they were facing. He stood, reaching out his hand to help her rise. Together, they moved through the cave, their breaths visible in the freezing air, their footsteps the only sound in the stillness. The storm outside had calmed for the moment, but the temperature had dropped even further, and the weight of the night seemed to press down on them both.

Outside the cave, the world was a frozen wasteland—silent and unyielding. The path they had chosen was dangerous, and their every step carried the weight of the kingdom's fate.

They pushed onward, the mountains ahead still shrouded in mystery, their peaks cutting into the sky like jagged teeth. But now, with each step they took, Lira felt the weight of the frost pressing down on them like a physical force, each breath of cold air reminding her of the danger they were in. The Queen's soldiers could be close—too close for comfort—and the shadow of the darkness that the Queen had spoken of loomed ever larger in her mind.

By the time they reached the foot of the temple, the night

had fully descended, leaving them with little visibility. The temple stood before them like a massive monolith, half-buried in the snow and ice, its dark stone walls marked with ancient runes that glowed faintly in the dim light. The air around the temple was thick with magic, a palpable presence that made Lira's skin crawl.

"We're here," Eryn said, his voice low as he surveyed the entrance to the temple. His hand tightened around the hilt of his sword, and Lira could sense the unease in him, despite the calmness in his voice. "This is where it all ends."

Lira nodded, her heart hammering in her chest. This was it. The culmination of everything they had done, the moment when they would either succeed or fail. The relic was inside. The answers, the power to end the winter, lay within the cold stone walls. But the price for failure was unimaginable.

The snow around them began to fall again, thickening in the air, swirling in the wind. It was as if the mountain itself was warning them to turn back. But Lira didn't hesitate. There was no turning back now. They had come too far.

Together, they stepped forward, into the temple's shadow.

Inside, the air was even colder, the walls lined with ice and stone, the faint glow of ancient runes illuminating the path ahead. The echoes of their footsteps seemed to carry for miles in the eerie silence. Each step felt like they were descending further into the heart of something ancient and forgotten, something that held both the key to their salvation and the power to destroy them.

They moved cautiously, each corner they turned filled with uncertainty. The temple seemed to stretch on endlessly, its passageways twisting and winding like a labyrinth. The air grew colder still, and Lira could feel a creeping dread in her chest, the weight of the magic pressing down on her, almost suffocating her. The relic was near, she could feel it. But so was the darkness.

Suddenly, they turned a corner, and the path ahead opened into a vast chamber, its walls adorned with intricate carvings of ice and stone, depicting battles long forgotten, gods and creatures that had once roamed the earth. In the center of the room, upon a raised platform, was the relic—a stone glowing with an eerie, unholy light, its energy pulsating like a heartbeat.

Lira's breath caught in her throat as she gazed at it. The relic. The source of the Queen's power. The key to the curse. And yet, as she stood there, her pulse quickening, she could feel the darkness—the weight of it—growing stronger with every step they took.

Eryn's voice was a whisper in the stillness. "We have to destroy it. Quickly."

Lira nodded, her body tense as she approached the relic, every instinct screaming at her to turn back, to run. But she didn't. She couldn't. The fate of Amara rested in her hands.

And then, as she reached out to touch the relic, a voice—low, guttural—echoed through the chamber.

"You are too late."

Lira froze. The air around them seemed to grow colder still, the magic in the temple shifting, swirling like a storm. The ground beneath their feet rumbled, and the walls seemed to close in.

The darkness was coming.

And they had no choice but to face it.

Ten

The Shattered Crown

The wind howled across the frozen plains, carrying with it the bitter sting of a winter that had lasted for centuries. The icy walls of Amara's capital were no longer a comforting symbol of safety—now, they were a prison. A cage of frost, one that the people could no longer bear. The rebellion was rising, and with it, the crackling, palpable tension that had long simmered beneath the surface of the kingdom.

Lira stood at the edge of the courtyard, her cloak drawn tightly around her, though it did little to keep the cold at bay. Her breath formed visible clouds in the frigid air, and yet, it was the gnawing weight in her chest that was the hardest to endure. The weight of the choices she had made. The truth that had been revealed. The burden of the knowledge that everything she thought she knew had been a lie.

The city below was in turmoil. Word of the rebellion's rise had spread like wildfire. Whispers of revolt filled the streets, while those loyal to the Queen patrolled in growing numbers. Even the soldiers who had once believed in her rule were now questioning their place in the kingdom.

Lira's heart pounded as she gazed out over the snowy landscape. Every corner of the kingdom was on the brink of change. It wasn't just the rebellion rising—it was something deeper, something far darker that had been unleashed. Eryn's voice echoed in her mind: *The darkness is waking, Lira. We've already set it free.*

She closed her eyes, trying to push away the gnawing fear. There was no going back now. The Queen had played her part in binding the darkness to the eternal winter, trapping herself in a cage of ice, and for centuries, the kingdom had known only the cold.

But the curse was no longer the only danger. The true cost of the Queen's reign was becoming clear. Lira could feel the weight of it, the knowledge that the Queen had sacrificed not just herself, but everything she had ever been, to keep the darkness at bay. And now, the choice between loyalty and love, between the truth and the lie, was becoming more unbearable by the moment.

Her eyes darted toward the shadows where Eryn stood, his tall frame silhouetted against the gray sky, his gaze fixed on the city below. He had been by her side through all of this— the secrets, the revelations, the journey into the heart of the mountains. Their bond had deepened with every passing day, and yet, it was becoming clear that the bond they shared would either save them or destroy them.

The air felt heavier, charged with something she couldn't name. She crossed the courtyard, her boots crunching in the snow, until she stood beside him. Eryn didn't turn to look at her, but his presence was a comfort she couldn't deny.

"What happens now?" she asked, her voice barely more than a whisper.

Eryn turned to her slowly, his eyes shadowed with something she couldn't quite decipher. The anger, the fear, the sorrow—it was all there, locked behind that calm exterior. "Now, we face the consequences of our actions. The Queen can no longer protect us, Lira. The darkness has been set free, and it will stop at nothing to reclaim the kingdom."

Lira felt a cold shiver run through her, but it wasn't the frost that had taken root in her chest—it was the truth. The realization that they had broken something that could never be fixed. They had thought they were freeing the kingdom, ending the eternal winter, but now they had unleashed the very force the Queen had tried to contain. They had made the darkness their own, and now, it was closing in on them.

"I don't know if I can do this anymore," Lira said, her voice trembling. She looked down at her hands, at the strength she had once felt, now slipping away like sand between her fingers. "The Queen... I thought she was our enemy. But now I understand—she trapped herself, didn't she? She trapped herself in the role of the Winter Queen, binding herself to the curse to keep the darkness from consuming us all."

Eryn didn't speak right away. His expression was unreadable, but there was something raw in his eyes, something that told her he was struggling with the same truths.

"Lira," he said finally, his voice quiet, "she did. She knew what the cost would be, but she did it anyway. She sacrificed her life, her humanity, to keep Amara safe. But it wasn't just her sacrifice—it was the entire kingdom. The people have lived in this prison of ice for so long, but they've been kept safe.

The Queen's power kept the darkness at bay, and now—now we've set it loose."

The weight of his words settled over her like a storm. The Queen's sacrifice had been for them. For Amara. But it had also bound her to the ice, to the curse of eternal winter. And now, Lira was faced with an impossible choice: to stand by the Queen, to preserve the balance that had kept them safe, even if it meant losing Eryn, or to risk everything—*everything*—to end the curse and fight for freedom, for love.

"Eryn…" Lira's voice broke, the name tasting bitter on her lips. "If we end the Queen's reign—if we destroy the curse—we destroy her, too. We destroy everything. *She* was the one who kept the darkness away. She was the one who kept Amara alive. What if we can't stop it? What if this rebellion… what if it isn't worth it?"

Eryn's eyes softened, his hand reaching for hers, and for a moment, Lira felt the warmth of his touch, the bond between them grounding her in the chaos. "We don't know what will happen, Lira. We never have. But if we don't try, if we don't fight to change things, then we're no better than the curse we sought to end."

Lira turned away from him, her heart torn in two. She wanted to be with him, to believe that the world they dreamed of was possible. But the truth was so much more complicated. The rebellion was already rising in the streets, the people were beginning to question everything, and the Queen's grip on the realm was slipping. But in the quiet corners of her heart, she still felt the weight of the Queen's sacrifice. The balance that had kept Amara safe for so long.

"I'm not sure I can betray everything I've ever known," Lira whispered, the words heavy with the gravity of her confession.

Eryn's voice was gentle, but there was a strength to it that held her in place. "You don't have to betray anything, Lira. You're not betraying the Queen—you're choosing what's right for the people. For Amara. The darkness she held back is rising, and we can't let it consume us all."

Lira turned to face him, her heart beating louder now, her mind spinning with the decision she had to make. She had spent so long serving the Queen, believing in her rule, in her strength. But now, in this moment, she realized that the Queen's power had been built on a lie. The winter, the curse— it wasn't protection. It was a prison.

"Then what are we supposed to do?" she asked, her voice hoarse. "What if we fail? What if the darkness is too strong? What if all we do is destroy everything we've fought for?"

Eryn reached out, his fingers brushing against her cheek, the touch soft but firm, grounding her in the moment. "We can't be afraid of what's to come, Lira. If we don't act now, if we don't stand together, then the darkness will win. Not just for us, but for everyone."

She closed her eyes, the weight of his words pressing down on her like a heavy stone. The rebellion was already gathering strength. The people were rising up, the forces of the Queen growing weaker with each passing day. And yet, in the midst of the storm, there was the quiet call of something greater—the promise of freedom, of a world where love and light could once again exist.

But could she really do it? Could she really choose to end the curse, to risk everything she had ever known?

"Eryn," she said quietly, her voice trembling. "What if we're not enough? What if this darkness is too great for us?"

Eryn's eyes softened with understanding. "We are enough,

Lira. Together. You've already chosen once. You chose to fight for what's right, for what's possible. And I will always be by your side, no matter what happens."

Tears welled in her eyes as she looked at him, the weight of his words breaking something inside her. She had spent so much time doubting, so much time questioning, but in the end, she knew the truth. The Queen had sacrificed everything to keep them safe, but now, it was their turn to fight. The rebellion was rising, the darkness was waking—but they had a choice. And they would face it together.

Lira took a deep breath, steadying herself. The road ahead was fraught with danger, with the possibility of losing everything. But it was also the only road that would lead to freedom.

"I'm ready," she said, her voice steady, her heart resolute. "Let's end this. Together."

And in that moment, as the wind howled around them, as the storm of rebellion raged outside, Lira knew there was no turning back. They would face whatever came next—together.

Lira and Eryn stood together, their hands clasped tightly, their resolve firm despite the storm that raged around them. The rebellion was rising, the Queen's rule was slipping, and the darkness—the force that the Queen had so carefully contained for centuries—was awakening. The weight of the choice that lay ahead pressed down on Lira's chest like a heavy stone, but she knew that there was no turning back. They had already crossed the point of no return.

They had made their decision. They would face whatever came next, together.

Eryn's eyes met hers, and in that moment, there was no more

fear in them, no more doubt. Only determination. "We need to act quickly," he said, his voice low and urgent. "The Queen's soldiers will be looking for us. The rebellion is gathering strength in the streets, but we can't afford to wait. We need to get to the heart of the capital—there's still a chance to stop this."

Lira nodded, the weight of the decision settling within her. The Queen's power had always been absolute, her icy rule unchallenged. But now, as the rebellion swelled in the streets, the balance had shifted. The Queen's kingdom was teetering on the edge of chaos, and Lira and Eryn were the ones who had the power to tip it in one direction or the other.

"We'll need to move fast," Lira said, her voice steady despite the storm in her chest. "The rebellion is already making its way into the capital, and the Queen's forces will be trying to put it down. If we're going to get to the heart of her power, we have to move before it's too late."

Eryn's jaw tightened as he glanced at the distant horizon, where the first light of dawn was beginning to pierce the dark clouds. The storm had not let up, but there was something in the air now—an electric tension, as though the very world was holding its breath. "We'll have to fight our way through," he said, his eyes meeting hers with a mix of determination and something darker. "The Queen won't just let us walk into her palace. We'll need to stay ahead of the soldiers."

Lira clenched her fists at her sides, her resolve solidifying. She had come this far, and there was no turning back now. The Queen had spent centuries building her rule on the curse of eternal winter, but now, it was time to bring an end to it. The cost of the Queen's power had always been too great, and Lira knew that it was up to her and Eryn to destroy what had been built on that sacrifice.

"Then let's go," she said, her voice low but resolute. "We'll make our way to the palace, and we'll destroy what's left of the Queen's power."

Without another word, they began their journey toward the heart of the capital, moving quickly through the snow-drenched streets. The city that had once felt like home now seemed foreign, twisted by the growing unrest that pulsed beneath its surface. The once-silent walls of the palace loomed ahead, the great structure of ice and stone standing as a reminder of the Queen's unyielding control over her people.

But as they moved closer to the palace, something shifted. The people of Amara, who had long lived under the Queen's rule, had begun to take notice. The streets, once still and silent, were now alive with whispers of revolt, with the sound of boots marching in the snow. Lira could hear the murmurs growing louder as they passed, the weight of the rebellion growing in the very air around them.

"They're rising," Eryn muttered under his breath, his eyes scanning the streets for any sign of danger. "The people are waking up. They know the truth now. The Queen's reign is over."

Lira's heart pounded as she glanced around, her senses alert to every movement, every sound. The world had shifted, and now they were in the eye of the storm. They had made their choice, but the battle ahead was far from over. The Queen's soldiers were closing in, and they would do whatever it took to protect the power that she had so carefully built. But the truth was now out, and the people were no longer afraid to stand against her.

They moved quickly through the streets, sticking to the

shadows, keeping their heads down. But even as they moved, Lira couldn't shake the feeling that they were being watched. The tension in the air was thick, oppressive, as if the city itself were holding its breath, waiting for something to happen. And then, they heard it.

A distant cry—a roar of fury, followed by the unmistakable sound of battle. The streets ahead were filled with smoke, the air thick with the sounds of clashing swords, the shouts of soldiers and rebels alike. The rebellion had reached its breaking point.

"They're here," Eryn said, his voice low but urgent. "We need to move faster."

Lira nodded, her heart racing as they sprinted through the streets, weaving through the crowds, keeping to the shadows. The capital had erupted into chaos, and now, they were caught in the middle of it. The rebellion was everywhere—voices raised in defiance, weapons drawn in protest—and the Queen's forces were fighting back with all their might.

As they neared the palace, the air seemed to grow colder, as if the walls themselves were closing in around them. The Queen's power was still alive, still hanging over the capital like a shadow. But with every step they took, they were getting closer to the heart of it. Closer to the truth.

And then, they reached the gates of the palace.

The great ice doors stood before them, towering and immovable, the cold radiating from them like a living force. Lira felt the weight of the moment pressing down on her as they stood before the gates. The Queen had always been the one to hold the key to Amara's fate, but now it was in their hands.

Eryn turned to her, his gaze steady and filled with determination. "This is it, Lira," he said. "We go in, we confront the

Queen, and we end this."

Lira swallowed, her heart pounding in her chest. The choice she had made—to stand by Eryn, to fight for freedom—had brought them here, to the edge of the Queen's power. But now, as she looked at the gates of the palace, she couldn't help but feel the weight of the sacrifice that had been made to keep them safe.

"We end this," Lira said, her voice barely a whisper, but full of conviction.

Together, they pushed open the gates, stepping into the heart of the Queen's domain.

Inside, the palace was dark, the cold walls lined with ancient tapestries and statues, each one an eerie reminder of the Queen's reign. The halls were empty, save for the sound of their footsteps echoing through the stone chambers. The power that had once filled this place now felt hollow, as though the very air was waiting for something to happen.

Lira could feel it—the darkness, the power that had been contained for so long. It was alive, thrumming beneath her feet, pulsing through the walls. The Queen's reign was ending, but the price of that end was unknown. The darkness was still there, still waiting, and they would have to face it.

They moved deeper into the palace, the silence broken only by their breath, the weight of the moment pressing down on them both. And then, they reached the throne room.

The doors were wide open, the vast chamber before them shrouded in shadows. At the far end, seated upon the throne of ice, was the Queen. She was no longer the powerful ruler who had once held the kingdom in an iron grip. She was a figure of defeat, her once-pristine robes now tattered and worn, her eyes darkened by the knowledge of what was to come.

Lira's heart caught in her chest as she met the Queen's gaze, the weight of their shared history between them. The Queen had been her mentor, her guide, the one who had raised her to be loyal. But now, they were enemies.

"Lira," the Queen said, her voice raspy, filled with something like sorrow. "You've come to end it all, haven't you?"

Lira didn't answer at first, her breath catching in her throat. There was so much to say, so much to confront. But all she could do was stand there, staring at the woman who had once been everything to her.

"We have to end it," Lira said finally, her voice filled with regret. "The winter has to end. The people can't live like this anymore."

The Queen's gaze softened for a moment, but it quickly hardened again, her voice cold and filled with finality. "You think you can destroy everything I've worked for? You think you can end the curse and save this kingdom?"

Lira stepped forward, her eyes filled with both sorrow and resolve. "I'm not doing this to destroy you. I'm doing this to save them."

The Queen's laugh was bitter, hollow, echoing through the empty throne room. "You don't understand, Lira. You can't undo what has been done. I have given everything for this kingdom. And now, you are too late."

The walls of the throne room began to tremble, and a low, ominous rumble filled the air. The darkness was rising again, and with it, the realization hit Lira: this wasn't just about the Queen. It was about Amara, and the choices that would either save or destroy them all.

The battle had begun.

Eleven

The First Flame

The winds howled as they climbed higher into the frozen mountains, biting into Lira's exposed skin, stinging her face and numbing her fingers. The terrain was unforgiving, the snow thick and deep, the cold so intense it seemed to seep into their very souls. The world around them was a vast expanse of white, as if they were walking through a landscape made of glass—fragile, shattering, and endless.

Eryn moved ahead of her, his strides steady, his eyes sharp as he scanned their surroundings. His presence, strong and unwavering, was the only thing that kept Lira grounded in the storm. The journey had worn on them both, but there was a fire within him, a determination that burned hotter than the cold around them.

Lira's thoughts, on the other hand, were a chaotic storm of their own. The bond between them, once a fragile thread, had grown stronger with every passing moment. Their love had become their strength, but it was also their weakness. They couldn't deny it any longer. The magic they were awakening, the ancient force tied to their very beings, was both a blessing and a curse. The power coursing through Lira's veins was intoxicating, yes, but it came with a price.

Her connection to the realm's magic had started to grow stronger since the destruction of the relic—the relic that had once tied the Winter Queen's power to the land. Lira had felt it in the depths of her soul, an ancient magic stirring within her, rising with every step they took toward the heart of the mountains. But as the power within her grew, so did the curse. It was like a living thing, breathing in her chest, gnawing at her insides, reminding her that this magic could not be used without cost.

Every time she called upon it, she felt the coldness within her deepen. It was as though the frost, once a barrier, had now become part of her. The world around her blurred in moments of power, and each time she used the magic, she felt a piece of herself slipping away. She had become the very thing she had once fought against—the embodiment of the curse she had sought to end.

And yet, she couldn't stop. She couldn't ignore the magic, not when it was so strong within her, not when she knew it was the only way they could save Amara.

Eryn glanced over his shoulder, his dark eyes locking with hers. "You're quiet today," he said, his voice barely rising above the wind. "What's on your mind?"

Lira met his gaze, her breath visible in the freezing air, but she didn't immediately answer. She couldn't. The truth was too heavy to speak aloud, and she wasn't sure she could explain it if she tried.

"I'm fine," she said at last, her voice hoarse from the cold. "Just… thinking."

Eryn didn't press her, though she could tell he wasn't convinced. He knew her too well by now. Still, he said nothing as he turned back to the path ahead. His gaze was focused, his jaw set in determination. They had a mission. The relic, the source of the Queen's power, lay ahead of them, and they were nearing the heart of the mountains where it had been hidden for centuries.

The weight of their journey pressed on them both, the unspoken knowledge that they were reaching the final stage of their quest. The relic was supposed to be their salvation, the key to breaking the curse. But Lira had seen too much to believe that anything came without sacrifice. They were close—so close—but with each step they took, the danger seemed to grow.

"Do you think we'll find it?" Lira asked after a long pause, her voice carrying the uncertainty she had buried deep inside her. "The relic… the magic that can end the winter?"

Eryn didn't turn back to her, but his answer came without hesitation. "I believe we will. The relic is the key. But there's more to it than we realize. We've come this far, Lira. We can't stop now."

The determination in his voice was enough to push her forward, but still, the unease in her chest gnawed at her. Every instinct screamed that something was waiting for them. Something far more dangerous than they had prepared for.

Finally, after what felt like an eternity of climbing through snowdrifts and ice, they reached the summit of the mountain. The wind screamed around them, but the cold was no longer the only thing that gripped them. Ahead, through the thick layers of snow and ice, was a cavern—a gaping maw in the rock that seemed to pulse with a dark energy.

"This is it," Eryn said, his voice a mixture of awe and caution. "The heart of the mountain. The relic is inside."

Lira stepped forward, feeling the magic within her stir in response to the cavern's pull. She could feel the power of the land here, as though the mountain itself was alive, waiting. Waiting for them.

Her heart thudded in her chest, but she didn't hesitate as she followed Eryn into the cavern. The darkness inside was thick, almost suffocating, and as they walked deeper into the heart of the mountain, Lira could feel the weight of it pressing in on them. The walls of the cavern were covered in ancient symbols, etched into the stone by long-forgotten hands. The air was thick with magic, the remnants of an old power that had been sealed away for centuries.

The further they ventured, the more Lira could feel it—the magic calling to her, pulling her toward something. But it wasn't just the relic. It was something else. Something darker.

Eryn stopped suddenly, his hand reaching out to grip her arm. His eyes were wide with alarm. "Do you feel that?" he asked, his voice low.

Lira nodded, the chill in her bones deepening. "It's… different. It's like the magic is alive, breathing."

The air around them seemed to shift, the temperature dropping further still. The walls of the cavern were closing in on them, and Lira's heart raced as she scanned the shadows, feeling the presence of something—something that didn't belong.

And then, from the darkness, it emerged.

It was a creature, something that had once been human, twisted by magic into a form of pure ice and shadow. Its eyes were hollow pits of darkness, and its body was made of living ice, shards of frozen death extending from its limbs. It stood tall, towering over them, and when it moved, the air seemed to freeze around it. The very essence of the creature seemed to suck the warmth from the air, the magic it exuded thick and suffocating.

Lira's breath caught in her throat, and she instinctively took a step back, her hand going to the hilt of her sword. But the creature did not attack. It simply stood there, watching them, its cold gaze fixed on Lira and Eryn.

"It guards the relic," Eryn whispered, his voice tight with tension. "We'll have to fight it."

Lira felt her pulse quicken, her hand tightening around the sword's hilt. The magic inside her stirred, a response to the creature's presence, but it was not the magic she was used to. It was darker, more intense, like a fire smoldering just beneath the surface. She could feel the pull of it—could feel the curse trying to rise within her, threatening to consume her.

But she couldn't let it. She wouldn't.

Lira drew her sword, the metal gleaming faintly in the dim light, but she didn't move. Not yet. She could feel the weight of the creature's gaze, and she knew that this battle would not be won with weapons alone.

Eryn moved to her side, his own sword drawn, his body tense. "Stay close," he murmured. "We need to stay together."

The creature's form shifted, a low growl reverberating from its chest, and then, in a blur of motion, it lunged at them.

Lira's instincts kicked in, and she barely managed to dodge the creature's strike. The cold air around them seemed to freeze in place as the creature swiped at her with jagged claws made of ice. She blocked the strike, but the force of the blow sent a shockwave through her body. The creature's strength was unimaginable, fueled by an ancient magic that was far stronger than anything she had ever encountered.

As the battle raged, Lira's heart pounded in her chest, her thoughts a blur. She was no longer just fighting for survival—she was fighting for control. The power within her was wild, untamed, and the creature's presence only seemed to make it worse. Every time she used the magic, it felt like she was feeding the curse. Every time she called upon the power, a part of her slipped further into the darkness.

And then, she felt it—a surge of warmth.

The first flame.

It burned within her, a bright, pure light that pushed back the ice and shadow, burning through the darkness like a beacon. It was a fire she had never known, a magic that was hers to command. She wasn't just a vessel for the curse anymore. She was something else—something powerful.

With a cry, she released the magic, and the light flared around her, illuminating the cavern with a searing blaze. The creature howled, recoiling from the warmth, but it was too late. Lira's power engulfed it, the flames burning through the ice and shadow, reducing the creature to nothing more than steam and smoke in the air.

The cavern was silent again, save for their ragged breaths. Lira's heart raced, her chest rising and falling with each breath. She had done it. But the cost—she could feel it. The magic inside her was still there, still swirling, but now it was something else. It wasn't just the curse. It was a fire, a flame that burned bright within her.

But it came with a price.

Lira collapsed to her knees, the weight of the power inside her overwhelming. Eryn was at her side in an instant, his hand on her shoulder, his voice filled with concern. "Lira? Are you alright?"

She could barely speak. The curse, the magic—it was more than she could handle. The cost of using this power was more than just the physical toll. She could feel it deep inside her—a price that was slowly becoming unbearable.

But she didn't tell him that. She couldn't. Not yet.

"We're not done yet," she whispered, her voice barely audible. "We have to keep going."

And together, they moved forward, deeper into the heart of the frozen mountain, knowing that the journey had only just begun. The relic, the magic—it was all tied to Lira now. And the price of its power was still unknown.

Lira's mind raced as she pushed herself to her feet, Eryn's steady presence a grounding force beside her. The warmth from the flames she had unleashed still lingered, but it was quickly fading, replaced by an aching cold that seeped deeper into her bones. Her breath came in shallow gasps, the weight of the magic she had used threatening to crush her. It was like a living thing inside her now—a force that demanded to be controlled, but one that felt almost impossible to tame.

Eryn's hand rested gently on her arm, steadying her. "Lira, are you sure you're all right?" His voice was low, filled with concern, but there was an urgency to it as well, a sense that time was running out.

She forced herself to stand taller, to push away the weakness that threatened to overtake her. The creature they had just destroyed was nothing compared to what lay ahead. The relic, the source of the Queen's power, was still within their grasp, but the darkness that had been unleashed—the very power that had corrupted the Queen and bound her to the curse for centuries—was still alive in the mountain. They had come so far, but they weren't done yet.

"I'm fine," she said, her voice hoarse but firm. "We have to keep moving."

Eryn didn't argue, though she could see the doubt in his eyes. He knew her better than anyone else, and he knew that something had changed within her. The magic had shifted, and with it, so had she. It was there, in the way her fingers trembled ever so slightly, in the way she could feel the pull of the magic even now, stirring deep inside her like a fire waiting to burn out of control.

"Then let's go," he said, his voice quiet but resolute. "We've come too far to stop now."

They moved deeper into the cavern, the cold growing more intense with each step. The walls of ice around them seemed to shimmer with an unnatural glow, the ancient runes carved into the stone flashing in and out of view as if they were alive. Lira could feel the magic in the air, thick and heavy, pressing down on her chest as they made their way toward the center of the cavern. The relic was close now—so close she could feel it tugging at her, calling to her.

As they turned a sharp corner in the cavern, they were met with a vast chamber, its ceiling so high it seemed to disappear into the blackness above. The air here was still, the quiet eerie and oppressive. The walls of the cavern were covered in thick ice, the crystal formations glistening in the dim light like frozen teeth. And in the center of the chamber, standing on a pedestal of ice, was the relic. It was smaller than Lira had imagined—just a simple stone, dark and smooth, its surface shimmering with an inner light that seemed to pulse with a life of its own.

But it wasn't just the relic that held her attention. It was what stood beside it.

A figure, cloaked in shadow, stood motionless beside the pedestal, its form draped in tattered, frozen robes. Its face was obscured, but Lira could feel its presence like a weight on her chest, a darkness that seemed to leech the warmth from the air around them. She couldn't explain it, but the creature—no, the being—was not entirely human. Its form flickered, half-melded with the shadows, its eyes glowing with an unsettling, otherworldly light.

"It's guarding the relic," Eryn said, his voice tight with the recognition of the threat before them.

Lira nodded slowly, her pulse quickening. She could feel the weight of the creature's gaze, even though its face was hidden from view. The power radiating off it was far greater than any magic she had ever felt. This wasn't just a guardian—it was a manifestation of the very force the Queen had bound herself to. The darkness, the curse that had shaped the fate of Amara for centuries.

The being's voice, when it came, was low and almost inaudible, a whisper that seemed to come from everywhere at once. "You seek the relic," it murmured, its voice like the cracking of ice. "But it is not for you to wield. You cannot control what has been bound."

Lira's heart skipped a beat. The words echoed through her mind, the weight of their meaning sinking deep into her chest. This being, whatever it was, knew them. Knew their purpose.

Knew their intentions. And it was warning them.

"The Queen—" Lira began, but the figure interrupted her, its voice cutting through her like a blade.

"The Queen is no more," it said, its voice reverberating off the icy walls. "Her sacrifice was hers alone, but it was not enough. The relic was never meant to be destroyed. It was meant to be *controlled*. And you—" The figure turned its head slightly, its unseen gaze locking onto Lira. "You are not its master."

Lira's breath caught in her throat. The creature's words were like a poisoned arrow aimed straight at her heart. The relic was never meant to be destroyed—it was meant to be controlled. She realized with sudden clarity that the Queen's power wasn't the key to breaking the curse; it was the key to controlling it. The Queen had trapped herself in the role of the Winter Queen to prevent the relic from falling into the wrong hands. But the truth was far more complicated. She had never intended to end the curse—she had only sought to keep it contained.

The being took a slow step forward, its form flickering in and out of shadow. "You are bound to the relic now," it said, its voice dark and dangerous. "Your souls are entwined with the magic that has kept this kingdom frozen. The cost of your actions will be more than you can bear."

Lira stepped back, her heart hammering in her chest. She could feel the heat of the magic inside her, rising, boiling under the surface of her skin. It was growing stronger, more uncontrollable, and with it, the curse seemed to awaken, as if responding to her fears.

"What are you?" she asked, her voice shaking despite her best efforts to steady it.

The figure moved closer, its form no longer hidden in shadow. It stepped into the dim light of the cavern, and Lira saw it clearly for the first time. It was no mere creature; it was a being born of the very magic that had shaped the kingdom. It had once been human, but now, its form was something beyond comprehension—part ice, part shadow, its body warped and twisted by centuries of bound power.

"I was once like you," it said, its voice echoing through the chamber. "I was once a keeper, a protector of the relic. But like all things tied to the power of the curse, I became something else. Something broken."

The words sent a chill down Lira's spine, and she felt the weight of the magic pressing down on her even harder now. She could feel the relic's call—the power inside her—growing stronger, louder, almost as if it were reaching out for the creature, for the being that had once been its keeper. The bond between her and the relic was undeniable now. She was its vessel, its conduit. And the more she used the magic, the more the darkness within her grew.

But it was not just the creature that made her fear. It was the growing sense of loss, of something slipping from her grasp. The more she embraced the magic, the more she felt herself disappearing into it. The darkness, the curse, was becoming a part of her. And with every breath, she could feel it taking hold, twisting her, pulling her deeper into the very heart of the power that had consumed Amara for centuries.

"We're not here to control it," Eryn said, his voice low but filled with resolve. "We're here to end it."

The figure tilted its head, a smile—or something like it—forming on its face. "You cannot end what has been bound for so long, child. You can no more break the chains than you can break the mountains themselves."

Lira's chest tightened as the figure's words struck home. The magic she had unleashed was tied to her, to her very soul. Every breath, every thought, every ounce of power she had used to fight the curse had only bound her more tightly to it. She could feel it now—something dark, something ancient, growing stronger within her with every moment.

"Eryn," she whispered, her voice trembling. "I can't. I can't control it."

But Eryn stepped closer, his hand resting gently on her arm. His eyes met hers, steady and unwavering. "You can, Lira. You've already started the fight. The curse is breaking. We just have to finish it."

The warmth of his touch anchored her for a brief moment, but the weight of the darkness inside her grew stronger, harder to ignore. She wanted to believe him. She wanted to believe they could still win, that they could still save Amara from the curse they had unleashed. But in her heart, she knew the truth: they were running out of time.

The figure in front of them took another step forward, its form solidifying, the shadows around it twisting like a storm. "You've come far, but you will not succeed. The relic will consume you, and you will become its new keeper. Like all before you."

Lira's breath caught in her throat, and her heart pounded in her chest as the creature's words sank in. It was true. She could feel it—feel the magic swirling around her, threatening to tear her apart, to pull her deeper into the very darkness that had been sealed away for so long.

And then, with a sudden surge of power, she reached out, her hand trembling as she touched the relic. The magic within her exploded, flooding the cavern with a brilliant, blinding light.

The creature screamed, its form disintegrating into shadow as the light engulfed it. But as the creature fell, so too did something within Lira. She could feel the curse unraveling, but in its place, there was something darker, something colder—a whisper, a promise, a price.

The first flame had ignited.

And with it, the world was changing.

Twelve

The Breaking of Winter

The cavern around them felt alive with energy, pulsing and vibrating with an ancient power that neither Lira nor Eryn had ever encountered before. The stone walls shimmered in the dim light, a surreal glow emanating from the ancient runes etched into the surface. The air was thick, heavy with magic, as if the very atmosphere itself were holding its breath. And at the heart of it all, the relic stood.

It was a simple stone, yet it radiated a sense of power that made Lira's chest tighten. It was the source of the Winter Queen's power, the key to the curse that had bound Amara in ice for centuries. But now, it was more than just a relic—it was an anchor, a bridge between the land of frost and the darkness that had been kept at bay for so long.

Lira could feel the pull of it, the dark, magnetic force that seemed to draw her in. It was like the relic was calling to her, beckoning her to step closer, to embrace its power. But with each step she took toward it, she could feel the curse within herself growing stronger, more insistent. The warmth she had once felt from the magic—the flames that had ignited within her—now felt like an insatiable fire, one that threatened to consume everything in its path.

Beside her, Eryn stood firm, his body tense, his eyes narrowed as he scanned the cavern, searching for any signs of danger. The creature that had once guarded the relic—the being born of ice and shadow—had been vanquished, its form reduced to nothingness in the wake of the light Lira had unleashed. But the danger wasn't over. Not yet.

"We're close," Eryn said, his voice low, his gaze flicking to the relic. "But there's something else here. Something waiting."

Lira nodded, feeling the weight of his words in her bones. She could feel it, too. The air had shifted, the atmosphere thickening as if something were waking up, something that had been dormant for far too long. The darkness that had once been kept at bay by the Queen's sacrifice was stirring, rippling like a wave about to break.

With a final, steadying breath, Lira stepped forward, her hand reaching for the relic. But as her fingers brushed against the cool stone, the world around her seemed to collapse.

The cavern shook with a violent tremor, the ground beneath their feet rumbling as a deafening roar filled the air. The relic pulsed with a dark, forbidding light, its power surging and crackling through the very air itself. Lira stumbled back, her heart racing as she tried to steady herself. The light from the relic was blinding, hot and cold all at once, a twisting, painful force that seemed to tear at her very soul.

Eryn grabbed her arm, his grip firm as he pulled her back. "Lira, don't—"

But it was too late.

The creature—the guardian of the relic—was not gone. It had only been waiting. And now, it was rising again.

From the darkness, the creature reformed, its body shifting and solidifying like liquid shadow, its form coalescing into something far more terrifying than before. This time, it was no longer just a manifestation of the curse—it was the embodiment of it. Its eyes, hollow and cold, locked onto Lira and Eryn, and the air grew colder still. The temperature dropped so sharply that Lira could see her breath form in the air, the frost freezing on the edges of her vision.

"You should not have come here," the creature growled, its voice like ice scraping against stone. "The curse cannot be broken. The Winter Queen's power is eternal. You cannot undo what has been bound for centuries."

Lira's heart pounded in her chest, the creature's words sinking deep into her mind like poison. It was right. The curse had been bound for so long. The Queen had sacrificed herself to keep it in place, and now, the creature—born of ice, shadow, and the curse itself—was determined to keep it that way. It would stop at nothing to preserve the power, to protect the balance that had kept the land frozen for so long.

But Lira knew something the creature didn't. The curse wasn't just a prison. It wasn't just a weapon. It was a chain. And now, Lira was the one who held the key.

With a final, shuddering breath, she stepped forward again, the darkness inside her rising, threatening to overtake her. The magic surged through her like fire, but it was cold—colder than anything she had ever felt before. She could feel the curse pulling at her, trying to claim her, to take over her very soul. She had always known there would be a price to pay for this power. She had always known there would be a cost.

And now, she understood it.

The creature charged at them, moving with terrifying speed. But Lira didn't flinch. She didn't step back. The power inside her, the magic she had unlocked, burned through her veins like molten fire. She could feel it—a flame growing brighter with every breath, hotter and more intense. The curse had always been inside her, and now, it was her to command.

She raised her hand, and the magic exploded out of her, surging forward in a torrent of light and heat. The creature screamed, its form writhing as the fire engulfed it, burning away the darkness that had once given it shape. But as the fire spread, so did the curse. Lira could feel it, a sharp pain in her chest, as though her very soul were being torn apart.

The creature was weakening, but so was she. The magic she had unleashed was too much, too powerful, and it was beginning to consume her from the inside. She could feel the frost creeping in again, the chill of the curse sliding beneath her skin. The warmth, the fire she had used to fight it, was fading.

Eryn's voice broke through the chaos, his words urgent and filled with fear. "Lira! You have to hold on! You can't let it take you!"

But Lira couldn't answer. She could barely hear him over the roar of the magic, over the deafening cry of the creature as it was consumed by the flames. The power inside her, the curse— it was suffocating her. She could feel herself slipping away, as though the magic was pulling her deeper into darkness.

With one final surge of effort, she reached for the relic, her hand trembling as she touched the cool stone once again. The light from the relic flared, blinding in its intensity, and for a moment, Lira thought she would be consumed by it. But then, something shifted. The warmth—the fire—surged once more, rising within her like a wave.

She closed her eyes, focusing on the power within her. She could feel the relic now, feel its pulse, its life force, tied to her own. The relic wasn't just a source of power—it was a part of the land itself, a force of nature that had been bound for centuries. But it was not invincible. Neither was she.

In that moment, Lira made the choice.

With a cry, she released everything—her life, her soul, the magic inside her—into the relic. The cost was unimaginable, but it was the only way. She could feel the curse unraveling, the frost dissolving as the warmth of the magic broke free. It was more than just fire now. It was light, it was life, it was the warmth of a world that had been locked in endless winter.

The relic shattered in a brilliant burst of light, the magic inside it imploding into the very core of the mountain. And as the light surged outward, the first rays of warmth touched the land. The frost began to melt, the ice cracking and breaking away, as if the earth itself was awakening from a long, cold sleep.

Lira gasped, the last remnants of her strength leaving her. She could feel the magic fading, the power slipping away from her, but it didn't matter. The curse was gone. The darkness was gone. The land was free.

As the light began to dim, Lira felt herself collapsing, her body trembling with exhaustion. She had given everything— her life force, her soul, her connection to the magic—and now, all that remained was the warmth that spread through the land, the first hints of spring in a kingdom that had been frozen for centuries.

Eryn was beside her in an instant, his arms wrapping around her as she fell into him, her strength gone. "Lira," he whispered, his voice thick with emotion. "You did it. You broke the curse."

Lira managed a faint smile, her eyes fluttering closed as the weight of her actions pressed down on her. "We did it," she whispered, her voice barely audible. "Together."

And in that moment, the first light of spring touched the land, and for the first time in centuries, the frost began to melt.

Lira's body felt like it was made of glass, fragile and shattering with every breath she took. She could barely focus on anything beyond the pulse of warmth that had begun to spread across the land, a warmth that was so foreign after centuries of winter. It seemed to seep into her very bones, wrapping around her like a blanket of light. But it wasn't just the warmth that she felt—it was the cost. The price of what she had given. The power, the life force, had drained from her so quickly that it felt like there was nothing left. Nothing but the echoes of what she had done.

She could hear Eryn's voice, distant at first, and then clearer as he held her against him. "Lira… please stay with me. Don't go. You've broken the curse, but I need you."

His words cut through the fog that was clouding her mind, and she felt his arms tighten around her, pulling her closer. She tried to open her eyes, but the effort was too much. Everything felt so heavy now. She could feel the warmth of his body against hers, the steadiness of his heartbeat, but it seemed to be fading, like a dream that was slipping through her fingers.

"Eryn…" she whispered, her voice barely audible, her lips trembling.

"I'm here, Lira. I'm right here," he reassured her, his hand gently brushing through her hair, trying to calm her, trying to keep her grounded in this moment. "Don't leave me, not now."

But she wasn't sure how much longer she could stay with him. She had given everything—her life, her magic, her very essence—and now it felt like the world was slipping away. The light from the broken relic had faded, but the warmth had remained, like the first rays of dawn creeping over the horizon, filling the world with the promise of life and hope.

Eryn's voice came again, this time more desperate. "Lira, please, stay with me."

She felt the last of her strength slipping through her fingers, like sand in the wind. She couldn't speak; she couldn't tell him that the cost was too great, that the price of breaking the curse was more than she could bear. But in her heart, she knew it was true. She had given everything for this moment, for Amara, for the world. But the sacrifice had been too much.

The land was healing. The first signs of spring were already appearing, the thaw spreading like a slow ripple through the mountains, through the very heart of Amara. The ice was melting, the rivers were flowing once more, and the trees—those that had stood frozen for centuries—were beginning to awaken, their buds beginning to stir.

But for Lira, the warmth that had once felt like salvation now felt like a cruel reminder of the life she was leaving behind.

Eryn held her tighter, his face pressed against her hair, his voice trembling with emotion. "Please, Lira. You've done it. You've saved us. Don't leave me."

For a moment, Lira gathered what little strength she had left, her eyes fluttering open to meet his gaze. She could see the pain in his eyes, the fear of losing her, and it broke something inside her, deep inside. She wanted to speak, to tell him that it would be okay, that they had done what they set out to do. But the words wouldn't come.

Instead, she reached for him with trembling fingers, her touch light against his skin. She felt her heart race, felt the warmth between them, and she allowed herself to feel the bond they had shared—the love that had sustained them through everything. Her strength was almost gone, but the love in her chest was still burning.

"I'm here," she whispered, her voice barely a breath, "I'm here... with you. Always."

And then, with a final, peaceful sigh, Lira closed her eyes, the warmth in her body flickering, flickering, and then fading into the cool embrace of the earth. The last remnants of the curse, of the ice that had once bound her, were gone. She could feel it—feel the land itself breathe a sigh of relief, as though a great weight had been lifted from the world.

For a moment, the world seemed to stop—frozen in time, a place between life and death. And then, the earth seemed to breathe once more, the air full of the promise of life.

Eryn's hands trembled as they held her, but he didn't let go. His voice broke through the silence, hoarse and filled with grief. "Lira... no. Don't go. Please."

And then, a miracle.

From the very depths of her being, a warmth began to stir again—faint, but undeniable. A spark, a flicker of life, a breath, a pulse. It wasn't the curse. It wasn't the magic that had threatened to consume her. It was something else, something that felt like hope.

Lira's chest rose slightly, her heartbeat a faint, distant thump. The warmth spread through her like sunlight breaking through dark clouds, a light that was both painful and beautiful. It wasn't the same as the fire she had released to break the curse—it was different, softer, more natural. It was her own.

Her fingers twitched against Eryn's chest, and his breath caught. "Lira?" he whispered, his voice trembling with disbelief.

With what little strength she had left, Lira smiled faintly, her eyes fluttering open. "Eryn," she breathed, her voice weak but full of determination. "I'm… here."

He didn't speak for a moment, and then, in a voice that was filled with relief and joy, he whispered, "You're alive."

Lira nodded slowly, her body still weak, but the warmth was spreading through her once more, reviving her, giving her strength. She could feel the pulse of magic inside her, the fire that had burned through her soul and the warmth that had healed the land. The relic had shattered, the curse was broken, and the land was free. But now, something had shifted within her.

Something new.

"I don't know how," she whispered, her voice barely audible, "but I think… I think I've found my place in all of this."

Eryn's hands cupped her face gently, his eyes filled with both wonder and fear. "Lira… You've done it. You've saved us."

Her heart ached with the depth of his words, but she knew they had done it. Together. They had broken the curse, they had ended the winter, and in that moment, she knew that their love had been the key to it all.

But there was something else—a flicker of power still inside her, a spark of magic that wasn't just about the curse. It was something more, something that had been awakened by the act of giving herself, of making that final sacrifice. The magic now pulsed within her, something that was uniquely hers, something that would never fade.

Lira slowly sat up, feeling the warmth of the land around her, the energy of spring—true spring—pushing through the air, warming the earth. The ice was melting around them, the frozen mountains beginning to thaw. The first light of dawn had touched the land, and the world, which had been locked in winter for so long, was finally breathing again.

Eryn stood beside her, his hand resting gently on her shoulder as he helped her to her feet. He was watching her closely, his eyes still filled with wonder. "You did it, Lira. You *did* it. We did it."

Lira smiled, her heart swelling with the weight of what they had accomplished together. The land was free. The darkness was gone. And the world was finally starting to thaw.

As they stood there, together, on the edge of the cavern, Lira could feel the warmth of the sun breaking through the sky, illuminating the world below them. The first light of spring touched the land for the first time in centuries, and the world seemed to awaken from its long, frozen slumber.

And as the warmth spread across the earth, Lira knew that it wasn't just the land that was changing. It was her, too. She had given everything, but in return, she had found her place in the world, and the magic that had once been a curse had become her strength.

Together, she and Eryn had broken the winter. Together, they would rebuild.

Thirteen

The Last Dawn

The first light of morning was unlike any that Lira had ever seen. It wasn't just the sun rising over the horizon, casting pale beams of gold and pink across the sky. It was something more—a warmth that stretched across the land, dissolving the remnants of the frozen night, cracking the icy veil that had once smothered everything. The air was fresh, alive with the scent of new growth, of soil and grass waking up after a long, bitter slumber. The earth, the trees, the very mountains themselves seemed to sigh with relief.

Lira stood at the edge of the forest, her breath still visible in the cool morning air, though she knew it wouldn't last. The thaw was moving fast now, faster than anyone had expected. The world around her was alive with transformation, the remnants of the winter slowly melting away, leaving behind a world that was both familiar and strange.

The curse had been broken. But the consequences—oh, the consequences—were only just beginning to unfold.

Eryn stood beside her, his eyes fixed on the distant horizon, his expression unreadable. She could feel the tension between them, thick as the rising mist. They had both sacrificed so much to reach this point, to shatter the Queen's power and end the eternal winter. But the price of that choice had not been clear. Not until now.

"Do you feel it?" Lira asked quietly, her voice barely more than a whisper. She didn't need to look at Eryn to know that he was feeling it too—the weight of the change, the tension that seemed to cling to everything. It wasn't just the land that was thawing; it was the people, the kingdom, the very fabric of Amara.

Eryn's jaw tightened as he exhaled slowly. "I do," he replied, his voice rough. "Things are… different. People are different. It's not just the winter that's ended, Lira. It's the old world. Everything's shifting."

She nodded slowly, her heart heavy in her chest. She had thought that breaking the curse would be the end of their fight, that the dawn of spring would be their victory. But now, standing here, with the first light of spring painting the world in shades of gold, she understood. The real battle had just begun.

The land was changing, yes, but so were the people. Those who had lived under the Queen's reign—the ones who had feared the winter but also relied on its unyielding grip for structure—were unsettled, unsure of what the world would look like without the cold, without the rigid control they had known for so long.

Eryn's voice broke through her thoughts, low and steady.

"The rebels are already stirring. Some want to embrace the change, to build something new. But others… they're clinging to the old ways. They don't trust what we've done. They don't believe in a future without the Queen's rule."

Lira turned to look at him then, meeting his gaze, and saw the same uncertainty mirrored in his eyes. He had always been the steady one, the one who believed in the cause, in the future they could build together. But now, even he seemed to be grappling with the enormity of the world they had set in motion.

"I never thought it would be like this," Lira confessed, her voice a mix of wonder and fear. "I thought breaking the curse would mean peace—freedom. But now… now it feels like we've opened a door, and everything's rushing in at once."

Eryn's expression softened, and he stepped closer to her, reaching out to take her hand. "We've given them a chance to choose, Lira. We've given them a new beginning. The world's never going to be the same, but that doesn't mean it's going to fall apart. We just have to help them rebuild."

Lira nodded, though doubt still lingered in her chest. Rebuilding—yes, they would rebuild. But the land they were standing on was fractured, torn between those who wanted to embrace the new dawn and those who wanted to cling to the old ways. The curse may have been broken, but the chains of tradition, fear, and control were not so easily shattered.

"We can't do it alone," she said, her gaze moving across the thawing landscape. The forest in the distance was already starting to sprout new buds, the bare branches beginning to show signs of life. But that wasn't all she saw. There were villages, towns, and cities beyond this forest, filled with people who didn't yet understand what the breaking of the curse meant for them. Some would see it as salvation. Others would see it as destruction.

"We don't have to do it alone," Eryn said, squeezing her hand. "We'll help them. We'll lead them. Together."

Lira felt a flicker of hope at his words, but it was quickly overshadowed by the thought of what lay ahead. How could they lead a people so divided, so uncertain of their place in a world that was no longer locked in endless winter? How could she, with the weight of the magic still heavy in her chest, bring balance to a kingdom that had known nothing but frost and fear for so long?

"I don't know if I'm strong enough for this, Eryn," she confessed, her voice trembling. "I've done what I had to do, but… I feel like the weight of the curse is still inside me. The magic—it's still there, inside me. It's part of me now. And I don't know what it will do to me if I keep using it."

Eryn's gaze softened, his hand lifting to gently cup her face. His thumb brushed against her cheek, a simple gesture, but one that anchored her in the storm of uncertainty swirling around them.

"You are stronger than you know, Lira," he said quietly. "You've already faced the darkness inside you. You've already broken the curse. The magic is part of you, yes. But so are you. You control it. Not the other way around."

Lira closed her eyes, letting his words wash over her, grounding her in the present. She wanted to believe him. She needed to believe him. But the truth was, she wasn't sure who she was anymore. She wasn't just a soldier, a protector, a servant of the Queen's will. She was something more now. She had seen the darkness, the depths of the curse, and she had fought it with everything she had. But the magic inside her, the power that had once consumed her, still lingered.

"You're right," she whispered, her voice shaky but determined. "I have to believe in myself. In us. We've done the impossible. We can do it again."

And yet, despite the strength she was trying to summon, she couldn't shake the feeling that the hardest part was yet to come.

The world was thawing. The first signs of spring were undeniable. But even in the warmth of the sun, there was a chill in the air. A chill that came not from the cold, but from the uncertainty of the world they had created. The realm had been freed from the ice, but the people were still trapped by their own fears. The curse had been broken, but now, a new challenge had risen—one that would test not only their love but their very ability to lead.

"We'll start with the people closest to us," Eryn said, his voice steady, his eyes burning with a determination that Lira had come to rely on. "The rebels, the leaders who are ready to embrace the change. Together, we can unite them, build a coalition that will stand strong in the face of whatever comes."

Lira nodded, her heart heavy but resolute. "We can't do it alone. We need the people to understand that this new world… it's theirs to shape. But they have to believe in it first."

Eryn smiled faintly. "They will. You've already shown them what's possible. We just have to help them see it, help them believe it."

Lira turned to face him fully, her heart swelling with the love and trust she had for him. He was right. They had to rebuild, and together, they would. But the road ahead was long, and the challenges they faced were not just external. There were forces at play within the realm, forces of tradition and fear, forces that would fight to keep the old ways in place. Even after the ice had melted, the kingdom was fractured, and it would take time, patience, and leadership to heal it.

She placed her hand over his, feeling the warmth of his touch against her skin. The love they shared, the bond they had forged, was stronger than the magic that had once controlled them. It was the one thing that would keep them together, keep them grounded, in the face of everything that was coming.

"I won't let you do this alone," she said, her voice filled with resolve. "I'll stand by you, no matter what comes."

Eryn smiled, his gaze softening. "We'll do this together. Always."

The first light of spring bathed them in its warmth, and for a moment, Lira allowed herself to believe that maybe, just maybe, they could build the future they had dreamed of.

The first true light of spring lingered on the horizon, casting long shadows that slowly turned golden. The air had softened, no longer biting and harsh, but warm, alive, and filled with the promise of something new. The remnants of winter, once a heavy blanket, now seemed like memories fading into the past. Lira could feel the subtle changes—how the ground beneath her feet had started to soften, how the buds on the trees were beginning to swell with life, how the scent of fresh earth mixed with the crispness of the morning air.

But the beauty of it all seemed distant, muted by the weight of what lay ahead. The land had been freed, yes, but there was no guarantee that the people who inhabited it would embrace that freedom. It was easy to see the thaw in the earth, but the thaw in people's hearts was something else entirely. For every villager who welcomed the end of the curse with open arms, there were those who feared it. The Queen's reign, oppressive as it had been, had provided a strange kind of order—a harsh, unyielding certainty.

Lira walked beside Eryn, their boots crunching on the fresh snow, the layers of ice still melting around them. They had a long way to go—literally and figuratively. Rebuilding Amara, leading the people into the new world that was now unfolding, was not something they could do alone. They needed allies. They needed strength. And, above all, they needed trust. But trust—trust in a new world, in the future they had fought for—was not easily given.

As they neared the first of the villages, a dark thought struck Lira: How could she ask the people to trust in this change when even she wasn't entirely sure what it meant? The warmth they had fought for, the light that now bathed the land, was a double-edged sword. It offered freedom, yes, but it also left them vulnerable. The world was not only waking—it was unraveling.

"Do you think they'll be ready for this?" she asked, her voice thick with uncertainty.

Eryn glanced at her, his jaw tight, his eyes filled with a flicker of doubt he hadn't shown before. "I think they will have no choice but to be. The curse is broken. The winter's grip is gone, and the land is already changing. They can either move forward with it or be left behind."

"But what if they want to stay behind?" Lira's voice trembled slightly. "What if they want the old ways back? The Queen's rule may have been harsh, but it was known. It was… predictable."

"I know," Eryn replied quietly. "I've thought about that, too. I've thought about what happens when the cold—when the winter—finally leaves us for good. It's easy to blame everything on the Queen. But there were people who were comfortable under her rule. People who had no reason to question it. And now… now they're being asked to change everything they know."

Lira swallowed hard, her thoughts swirling. The rebellion had brought down a kingdom, but in its place was nothing but chaos. The pieces were all scattered, and though the winter had ended, the seeds of conflict had been planted in its place. People feared change, and what they didn't understand, they fought. Her heart clenched with the knowledge that she and Eryn were standing at the threshold of something vast and wild, something neither of them could control.

"Do you think we're ready for this?" she asked him softly.

Eryn squeezed her hand, his gaze steady but full of the same uncertain resolve she felt within herself. "I don't know. But we're all they have left. If we don't lead them, someone else will. And that will only make it worse."

They walked in silence for a while, the wind carrying the scent of fresh earth and the faint sound of birdsong—an odd thing in a land that had known only the harsh winds of winter. Lira could hear the distant murmur of people, the bustle of village life, but it was still early. The world felt new, fragile in its newfound warmth. She wanted to feel the promise of it, wanted to believe that they were stepping into a future where people could be free from fear and oppression. But it was hard to shed the weight of everything that had come before.

They reached the village at the base of the mountain just as the sun broke free from the clouds, bathing the village square in light. The small buildings of stone and wood were still covered in patches of snow, but the scent of fresh bread and warm fires filled the air. There were people here, ordinary folk—farmers, traders, families—living their lives in the shadow of the mountains. But as Lira and Eryn stepped into the square, a strange stillness seemed to fall over the crowd. Eyes turned toward them, silent, waiting.

It wasn't the reception they had expected, but it was the one they had prepared for. The land was thawing, but the hearts of the people had not yet followed suit.

Lira could feel their eyes on her, judgment hidden behind their silence. The Queen's legacy was still alive in their minds. Her presence had shaped their world for so long. She was more than a ruler. She had been a symbol, a constant—someone who had ensured that the world remained under control, even if that control was suffocating.

"You can't just undo centuries of fear and tradition with a single act, Lira," Eryn said, his voice low. "This is going to take time. They don't trust us yet."

Lira nodded, knowing he was right. She could feel it in the way they looked at her, at him—skeptical, guarded. The wind seemed to pick up again, biting at their faces as they made their way deeper into the village. Lira's thoughts swirled as she tried to understand what she needed to say, what she needed to do to break through the barriers of fear that still gripped the hearts of these people.

"Lira! Eryn!"

A voice called out, cutting through the air, and they both turned in unison to see a familiar face emerging from the crowd. It was Naida, a member of the rebellion, her face tired but determined, a deep sense of urgency in her eyes.

"They're gathering," she said breathlessly, running up to them. "The council—those who still cling to the old ways.

They're planning to fight this change. They want the winter back, the order the Queen gave them. They're not ready for a world without control."

Lira's heart sank. It was worse than she thought. The fear was not just in the hearts of the common folk. It was in the halls of power, too. Even now, those who had benefited from the Queen's iron grip on the kingdom were not willing to let it go.

"Where are they?" Eryn asked, his tone sharp with urgency.

Naida nodded toward the town hall—a small stone building near the village center. "Inside. They're debating whether to resist. They're afraid of what the thaw means."

Lira felt the weight of Naida's words in her chest. The kingdom was splintering. The land was thawing, yes, but the foundations of everything they had known were cracking beneath their feet.

"Lead the way," Lira said, her voice filled with determination. "We're not letting them take this from us."

As they moved toward the town hall, Lira could feel the unease rising inside her. She had thought that the battle against the Queen had been the hardest part of this journey. But now, she realized that the true challenge was just beginning. The curse may have been broken, but the chains of fear and tradition were not so easily undone.

They entered the town hall, its heavy wooden doors creaking in protest as they pushed them open. Inside, the air was thick with tension. A group of men and women sat at a long wooden table, their faces drawn with anxiety, their voices low but heated.

As soon as they entered, all eyes turned to them, and the room fell silent.

"Lira… Eryn…" A man at the head of the table, one of the village leaders, stood up slowly, his face hard and suspicious. "We didn't think you would show up. We thought you would be here to finish what you started—to bring us into some… unrecognizable future."

Lira stepped forward, her heart hammering in her chest. "We're here to help you understand. The winter is gone. The Queen's power is broken. But that doesn't mean we're leaving you behind. We're trying to rebuild—together."

The man's eyes narrowed, and he crossed his arms over his chest. "Rebuild? How can we rebuild when we don't know what comes next? We've lived under the Queen's rule for generations. We've survived this long with the winter. And now you want us to trust you? To believe that this new world you're talking about won't tear everything apart?"

Eryn's voice was sharp, his anger barely contained. "The world is already torn apart. The winter was just a bandage over a wound that's been festering for centuries. The old ways are gone. You can either fight it, or you can move forward."

Lira felt the tension between them all thickening, the room heavy with the weight of a thousand unspoken questions. The people in this room were scared. They had lived under the Queen's control for so long that they didn't know who they were without it. But they had a choice now. And that choice—whether to embrace the new world or cling to the past—was the hardest one they would ever face.

She looked around the room, meeting each person's eyes. "The curse is broken. You can either stay in the shadows of the past, or you can join us in the light of this new dawn."

There was a long silence.

And then, one by one, the heads of the council nodded, their expressions slowly changing from suspicion to something else. Something that might be hope.

"We'll need time," the village leader said, his voice gruff but not without respect. "But… maybe you're right. Maybe it's time to move forward."

The air in the room shifted, and for the first time, Lira felt a flicker of the hope she had been longing for. The land was thawing. And maybe, just maybe, the people would, too.

As they left the town hall, Eryn beside her, Lira allowed herself to believe that the change they had fought for—despite the struggles ahead—was still within their reach.

The Fire and the Ice

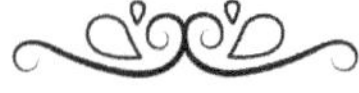

The sun dipped low behind the mountains, casting long shadows over the land. The snow that had once covered the earth like a heavy blanket was beginning to fade, replaced by the first signs of spring. Yet, for all the warmth that the thaw had brought, a chill still lingered in the air—a palpable tension that clung to the land like an unseen force.

Lira stood at the edge of a cliff, her eyes scanning the horizon. The world was changing—had changed—but something in her gut told her that the hardest part of this battle was yet to come. The fire they had set alight to break the curse had ignited something else, something far darker. Even now, she could feel it, lurking just beneath the surface, like a storm waiting to break.

Beside her, Eryn stood with his arms crossed, his gaze fixed on the same distant line of mountains that marked the boundary of the kingdom. His expression was unreadable, but the tension in his posture spoke volumes. He, too, could sense the threat that hung in the air.

"We've done everything we can," Lira said quietly, her voice carrying the weight of the uncertainty they both felt. "We've freed the land, broken the curse, and brought the people into the light. But there are still those who want the darkness back."

Eryn didn't answer immediately, his lips tight as he studied the horizon. "There are always those who will cling to the past. To power. To control."

Lira's fingers tightened around the hilt of her sword, the cold steel grounding her. "But it's more than that. It's like something is awakening. Something more dangerous than anything we've faced."

Eryn's gaze flickered toward her, his eyes dark with concern. "You think the darkness is still alive?"

"I know it is." Lira's voice was firm, but the truth of it made her insides twist with unease. "When we broke the relic, we didn't just break the Queen's power. We broke the balance she kept. And something—*someone*—is using that to rise again."

Eryn's brow furrowed as he stepped closer to her, his hand brushing lightly against hers. "We've faced darkness before. We've beaten it. Together."

Lira's eyes locked with his, a spark of hope flickering in her chest at his words. But that hope was fleeting, as the shadows of doubt crept back in. "We're not the only ones fighting for control now, Eryn. There are new enemies, ones who want to take what we've built and tear it down. The world is divided."

Eryn's lips tightened, and for the first time, Lira saw the weight of his own doubts reflected in his eyes. The fires they had ignited—the fires of rebellion, of freedom—had burned down the walls of the old world. But now, those flames had scattered, and the ashes were settling into something that could be as destructive as the ice they had so carefully destroyed.

Lira turned back to face the valley below, her eyes sweeping across the land. The rivers had thawed, the trees had begun to bloom again, but the fractured kingdom still bore the scars of centuries of cold rule. The people who had once lived in fear of the Queen's reign were now free, but they were also lost. Some were eager to embrace the change, to build something new from the ruins, while others clung to the old ways—driven by the belief that the order they had once known was better than the uncertainty of the world ahead.

Behind her, the sound of footsteps echoed in the quiet. Lira didn't have to turn around to know who it was. Naida, a fierce rebel and one of their closest allies, approached with her usual determined stride. Her eyes were sharp, her expression grim.

"It's worse than we thought," Naida said without preamble, her voice tinged with worry. "There are whispers. Rumors. Some of the old guard—the ones who served under the Queen—are rallying in the mountains. They want to return to the old ways, bring back the rule of the Winter Queen. They believe that the land is too wild without her control."

Lira felt a cold knot tighten in her stomach. She had known there would be resistance, but this… this was different. These weren't just rebels who wanted change. These were people who had been part of the old order, who had thrived under the ice, who couldn't fathom a world without it.

"They want power," Eryn said, his voice cold, his jaw clenched. "The curse may be broken, but some people can't let go of the chains they've lived under. They're afraid of losing what they once had—control, order. They think the thaw will destroy them."

Naida nodded, her face hardening. "They're not just sitting idly by, though. They've gathered a force. Small, but growing. They're using the old symbols—the relic's power. It's not just a rebellion anymore. It's a war for the soul of Amara."

Lira's heart sank at her words. She had hoped that the breaking of the curse would bring peace, but she had known deep down that peace was never simple. The people were fractured, and now, there were those who would fight to bring the winter back, to restore the Queen's control, even if it meant plunging the world into darkness once more.

"What do we do?" Lira asked, her voice barely above a whisper. She already knew the answer, but the weight of the question still pressed down on her like a stone.

"We fight," Naida said, her voice hardening with resolve. "We've already fought for this world once. We'll fight again. But we need to move quickly. If we wait too long, the enemy will have time to organize. We can't let that happen."

Eryn's hand found Lira's again, his grip firm. "We'll fight," he agreed. "Together."

Lira nodded, her throat tight with emotion. She had fought to free Amara, to bring an end to the Queen's reign, and she would fight again—this time for the world they had created, for the future they had built. But as the first light of spring bathed the land, she knew that the battle they were about to face would be unlike any they had fought before. The flames they had ignited had awakened something ancient and dangerous. And this time, the fire and the ice would meet head-on, with the fate of the kingdom hanging in the balance.

The days that followed were filled with the urgency of preparing for war. The people of Amara, those who had once been freed from the Queen's ice, now found themselves once more caught between the fires of rebellion and the cold shadows of their past. Lira and Eryn, along with Naida and their closest allies, gathered in the heart of the rebellion's camp, strategizing their next move. Tensions were high. The people who had fought for freedom were now faced with a fight they hadn't expected: the battle to maintain that freedom.

As they gathered around the table, maps spread out before them, the air thick with the sound of hushed voices, Lira couldn't shake the feeling that the darkness was growing closer. The whispers of the old guard were turning into something more—a rising tide that threatened to overtake them all.

"We can't let them take the mountains," Naida said firmly, her finger tapping the map where the old strongholds lay. "If they control the high ground, they'll be able to cut off our supply lines, crush any hope of a fight before it even begins."

"They won't be expecting us to strike first," Eryn said, his eyes scanning the map with calculated precision. "We'll use the element of surprise. If we move quickly, we can take their stronghold before they have a chance to rally more forces."

Lira felt the weight of their plans pressing down on her, the responsibility for the lives of those who had placed their trust in them heavier than ever. She knew the stakes. If they didn't act now, the darkness that had been awakened would destroy everything they had fought for. But the idea of leading their people into another war… another fight for survival… was almost too much to bear.

"What about the villages?" Lira asked, her voice low. "There are people in the towns who still fear what's happened, who fear the thaw. What do we do with them?"

Naida's eyes flickered with something between sympathy

and grim determination. "They'll have to choose. Those who want to fight with us will fight. Those who don't—well, we can't protect them forever."

Lira's heart tightened at the thought, but she knew there was no easy answer. The world was no longer divided just by ice—it was divided by fear, by mistrust, and by the fractured ideals of a kingdom that had known only winter for far too long. The battle ahead wouldn't be won by force alone. They needed the people to believe in the future they had fought for, to believe that the fire they had ignited was worth saving.

"Let's move out at dawn," Lira said, her voice resolute. "We fight for the land we've freed. We fight for the future we've built. And we will not let the darkness take that from us."

The fire and the ice were about to collide. The stakes had never been higher, and the cost of failure had never been clearer. The world was changing, and so were they. Together, Lira and Eryn would lead their people into a new age—one forged in the heat of battle and the cold of uncertainty.

The dawn was breaking, but so was the storm. And when the fire and the ice collided, nothing would ever be the same again.

The air was thick with anticipation as dawn broke over the horizon, casting a pale golden light across the camp. The sounds of the waking world felt muted under the weight of the battle that was about to unfold. Lira stood near the edge of their camp, her eyes tracing the first signs of light peeking over the distant mountains. The warmth of the sun was welcome, but it only made the tension in the air feel sharper, more tangible. She could hear the soft rustling of her comrades around her, preparing for the battle ahead.

Her armor felt heavier than usual, as if the very weight of the world was pressing down on her. Her heart raced, her thoughts swarming like bees trapped in a jar. She had thought that breaking the curse would bring peace, a new era of light. But instead, they were fighting again—not just for freedom, but for their survival, for the fragile hope that the thaw would bring.

As Eryn approached, Lira turned to face him, her eyes searching his. His expression was steely, his gaze fixed on the horizon, but there was something in the way his jaw clenched that told her he was feeling the weight of it all too.

"You're ready?" she asked, her voice a quiet whisper amidst the bustle of the camp.

Eryn's lips pressed into a thin line as he nodded. "I don't think any of us are ever truly ready for something like this. But we don't have a choice." His voice held a note of finality, a certainty that Lira wished she could feel herself.

"I'm not sure I'm ready either," she admitted, her voice tinged with the exhaustion that had built over the weeks since the battle to break the curse. "What if we're making a mistake? What if the people who want to return to the old ways... what if they're right?"

Eryn's gaze softened, and he stepped closer, taking her hand in his. His touch was warm, grounding her in the present, despite the chaos that loomed just beyond the camp's edge.

"They're not right," he said gently, his voice firm but full of compassion. "We've seen the old ways, Lira. We've seen the fear, the cold, the control. The people who are rallying behind the old guard—they're scared. They're clinging to what they know because they don't understand the power of what we've set in motion."

Lira swallowed, her throat tight. She had seen it—the fear in the eyes of the people, the uncertainty in the villages as the thaw spread. Some welcomed it, embraced the change, but others feared the unknown, the loss of everything they had once known.

"Then why does it feel like the old world is fighting back?" she murmured, looking down at the sword strapped to her side. "Why does it feel like we're the ones being torn apart?"

Eryn took her chin in his hand, lifting her face to meet his gaze. His eyes were soft, yet filled with an unshakable resolve. "Because the old world will fight to survive. But we've already broken the chains. We've already set them free. And we're going to make them see that the future we're fighting for is worth more than the past they're trying to hold on to."

Lira closed her eyes for a moment, letting the steadiness of his touch reassure her. He was right. The past was a shadow that would forever linger, but they had already chosen the path forward. They had broken the curse, torn down the walls that had bound the land in ice. Now, they had to rebuild.

"Let's go," she said, her voice firm with new purpose. "It's time."

They mounted their horses, and as the camp began to stir with the noise of preparation, Lira could feel the weight of the coming battle settling over her. She looked around at the faces of the soldiers, the rebels, the farmers and traders who had come together to fight for the world they had only begun to understand. There was fear in their eyes, but there was also hope—a glimmer of belief that this new dawn, this new world, could be theirs.

The roads were still covered in patches of snow, but the thaw had made everything feel more alive. Lira could see the greenery creeping out of the soil, the first flowers poking through the cold earth. It was a sign of renewal, of the world waking up after a long, endless winter. Yet, as the army set out, she couldn't shake the feeling that they were walking into the heart of the storm.

The march through the valley was quiet, the soldiers moving in tense silence, eyes darting between the towering peaks of the mountains and the scattered villages that lay in their wake. The landscape that had once been so cold, so unforgiving, now seemed filled with contradictions. The snow still clung to the highest peaks, but the valleys below were already changing—moss and new growth creeping up the sides of the rocks, streams running where they had once been frozen solid.

Lira felt a flicker of hope deep inside her chest, but it was quickly replaced by unease. Even the warmth of the thaw seemed to have a bite to it, like the land was not yet ready to accept the change. The air around them seemed to hum with the tension, as if the world itself were holding its breath.

As they neared the mountains, Lira could see the dark figures of the old guard—those who had once been the Queen's most trusted officers—gathering on the horizon. They had set up camp in a narrow pass, a natural barrier that provided them with a perfect vantage point. It was clear that they had been preparing for this moment, waiting for the thaw to give them an opportunity to seize control.

"They're waiting for us," Eryn said, his voice low but filled with the same steely resolve that she had come to rely on. "They know we're coming."

Lira nodded, her heart racing. "They won't just surrender, will they?"

"No," he replied, his eyes narrowing as he assessed their

position. "They're fighting for everything they once had. For power. For control. And they'll stop at nothing to take it back."

Lira took a deep breath, feeling the weight of the decision ahead of them. The old guard—those who had been loyal to the Queen's reign—had rallied against them, using the relic's power as their banner. The battle ahead wouldn't be just a fight for control of the land—it would be a fight for the future. The old world would either give way to the new, or it would tear it apart in an effort to preserve what it knew.

"We have to move quickly," Naida said, pulling her horse up alongside Lira's. "If we don't take them by surprise, they'll have the advantage. The pass is narrow. We'll have to use that to our advantage."

Lira looked out over the land, her mind racing. The plan was simple—move quickly, cut through their defenses, and take the stronghold before the old guard could mobilize their full force. But the land was still thawing, the terrain treacherous, and every moment they wasted was a moment their enemies could use to strengthen their position.

"We move at first light," Lira said, her voice steady with determination. "We fight for the future we've created. And we won't let them take it from us."

Eryn squeezed her hand briefly before he turned his gaze back to the mountain pass. His expression was a mirror of hers—determined, but with a flicker of something deeper. They had already fought the battle that mattered most. Now, they would fight for what came after.

The next morning, the air was thick with tension as the first light of dawn lit the sky. Lira and Eryn, leading their soldiers, moved toward the pass with the speed of a force unrelenting. They knew what awaited them—an army that was just as desperate, just as hungry for power, but they also knew that they had something their enemies didn't.

They had each other. And they had the future.

As they entered the pass, the first volley of arrows sliced through the air, and the ground trembled with the sound of battle. The fire and the ice were meeting head-on.

The world was still waking, still shifting, and nothing would ever be the same again.

Lira's sword flashed in the early light, and as she plunged into the fray, she could hear Eryn's voice, strong and commanding, cutting through the chaos. Together, they would face the darkness once more—and this time, they would emerge victorious.

Fifteen

The Price of Sacrifice

The land had begun to thaw, but not in a way that Lira had imagined. She had felt the weight of the sacrifice—the giving of her life force to the relic, the magic that had shattered the curse and set the world free from the ice. She had believed that the thaw would be complete—that the world would warm and grow, leaving behind the long winter. Yet, something was wrong. The air was heavy, thick with an unease that none of them could shake.

Lira stood at the edge of the forest, looking out over the valley that stretched below, the first signs of green creeping through the dirt. The sky was streaked with clouds, but there was no warmth to the sunlight. It was a strange, faint glow, like the sun was afraid to fully shine. The winds whispered through the trees, cold in the evening light. The seasons were shifting, yes, but the cold had not entirely released its grip.

She had sacrificed part of herself to break the curse—part

of her soul, her very essence—believing it was the only way. She had seen the land warm, the ice begin to crack, but now, she felt it—a chilling, creeping cold that came in waves. It was subtle at first, like a breath that came too quickly, like a shadow at the edge of her vision. And then it would pass, leaving behind a faint but unmistakable trace of winter's bite.

She closed her eyes, her breath visible in the cold air, but she knew it wasn't just the remnants of the old winter. Something was wrong. The magic that had been released, the ancient power that had once been bound to the relic, had altered the balance. They had freed the land from the Queen's reign, but in doing so, had awakened something much older, something much darker.

Lira could feel it in her bones. The cold had not gone, not entirely. It was lingering, hiding, waiting to strike again. It was as though the land itself was holding its breath, unsure of what to do next. The thaw had started, but there were strange fluctuations—times when the chill would settle in, like a warning that the curse was not truly gone. The land was still shifting, and no one understood why.

"Lira."

Eryn's voice broke through her thoughts, and she turned to find him approaching, his expression grim. His hair, once tousled by the wind, now hung flat against his face, the same chill that had swept through the land beginning to settle in his features.

"Eryn," she said, her voice soft but filled with a growing concern. "It's happening again."

He stepped closer, his eyes searching hers. There was something in his gaze, something that held both the weight of the world and the uncertainty of what was to come. "The cold.

I feel it too."

Lira nodded. "It's not just the weather, Eryn. There's something else. The magic we unlocked… it's not stable. The winter isn't truly gone. It keeps creeping back, like it's fighting to stay."

Eryn clenched his jaw, his fists tightening at his sides. "We broke the curse. We freed the land. This should be the beginning of a new age."

"But it's not." Her voice trembled with frustration. "The curse may be gone, but something else has awoken. Something ancient. The relic wasn't just a source of the Queen's power—it was a piece of something older. Something we didn't understand."

Eryn's brow furrowed, and he took a step forward, placing a hand on her shoulder. "What are you saying, Lira?"

"I'm saying the magic we unleashed wasn't just the end of the winter—it was the beginning of something else," she replied, her voice shaking as the realization settled in her chest. "I feel it, Eryn. The land is unstable. The cold is coming back, and I think it's connected to what we did. To what *I* did."

A flash of concern crossed Eryn's face, but it was quickly replaced by determination. "What do you want to do?"

"We need answers," Lira said, her voice steadying as she met his gaze. "We need to understand what we've awoken. If we don't, we risk losing everything we fought for."

Eryn nodded. "Then we'll find out together."

Lira turned back to the valley below, her eyes scanning the landscape. The air was heavy with the weight of their words, the stillness settling like a blanket around them. She could feel the pull of the cold, like a whisper that called to her from the distance. It was subtle, but it was there. The old world was not yet fully gone, and the price of their freedom had not yet been fully paid.

The journey to the ancient ruins where they believed the answers might lie was slow, treacherous, and filled with an ever-growing sense of unease. As they traveled deeper into the wilderness, the land around them began to shift in strange ways. Where the thaw had been swift and all-encompassing in some places, there were others where the snow still clung to the trees, stubborn and unmoving. The further they ventured, the colder the air became, until they found themselves in the heart of a dense forest where the very trees seemed to whisper in the wind.

"We're close," Eryn said, his voice tight with focus. He had been navigating through the rugged terrain with a sense of purpose, as if he knew exactly where they needed to go. "The ruins are just ahead."

Lira nodded, but her thoughts were elsewhere. She couldn't shake the sense that something was watching them, waiting for them to make the wrong move. The darkness that had been dormant for centuries was no longer passive—it was growing, pressing in on them, and she didn't know if they could stop it.

As they reached the clearing that marked the entrance to the ruins, Lira felt the magic around them shift, the air crackling with an unseen energy. She looked around, her breath catching in her throat as her eyes scanned the ancient stone structures, half-buried in snow. This was where the Queen had once drawn her power, where the relic had been locked away for centuries. But now, it was silent—eerily so.

Eryn stepped forward, his hand on the hilt of his sword. "This is it."

Lira's heart beat faster, the silence pressing in on her like a weight. They had come for answers, but what would they find in these ruins? The land had been changed by the magic they had unlocked, but they still didn't understand the true consequences. She could feel the tug of the darkness in the air, a subtle, persistent whisper that told her they were not alone.

"Stay alert," Lira warned, her voice low. "I can feel something."

Eryn nodded, his eyes scanning their surroundings as they made their way deeper into the ruins. The ancient stones were covered in moss and ice, worn by time but still standing tall, a testament to the forgotten power that had once flowed through them. The deeper they went, the colder the air became, until they reached the center of the ruins—a great circular chamber, its floor covered in thick layers of snow and frost.

In the center of the chamber, there was an altar. The stone was cracked, weathered by centuries of neglect, but it still held a strange power. Lira could feel it, pulsing beneath the surface, as though the magic of the land itself was still tied to this place.

"This is where it all began," Eryn said, his voice barely above a whisper. "This is where the Queen drew her power."

Lira stepped closer to the altar, her hand outstretched, and the cold magic seemed to swirl around her, pulling her in. "What happened here?" she asked, her voice barely audible. "Why did the Queen bind herself to this place?"

Eryn watched her, his eyes dark with concern. "She didn't just bind herself, Lira. She bound something else. The very essence of winter. The magic here isn't just about the cold—it's about control. The Queen's power was never about freedom. It was about holding everything in place, about stopping the world from changing."

Lira felt a shiver run down her spine as the truth began to

unfold. The relic had been a symbol of control, a way to keep the world frozen, locked in place. But now, that control had been broken—and the world was not prepared for the shift that had come.

"We need to destroy this place," Lira said, her voice steady despite the rising fear in her chest. "We need to sever the connection."

Eryn moved to stand beside her, his face grim. "We don't even know what that would do. What if it makes everything worse?"

Lira took a deep breath, the cold air stinging her lungs. "We can't live in the shadow of the past any longer. We've already fought for freedom. It's time to finish this."

Without another word, she reached forward, her hand brushing against the cold stone. The magic flared, swirling around her in a violent, crackling wave. The temperature plummeted, the air around them turning icy as a dark force began to coalesce.

Lira's heart raced as the ground beneath her feet trembled. The shadows began to rise from the stone, swirling into a dark shape—a figure cloaked in shadow, its eyes glowing with a cold fire.

"You should have left this place alone," the figure hissed, its voice a low, guttural sound that made Lira's skin crawl. "You think you can destroy what has been bound for centuries? You think you can sever the connection between the land and the cold?"

Lira stepped back, the magic inside her flaring to life as she braced herself for what was coming. "We already have. The curse is broken."

The figure laughed, a sound like ice cracking. "The curse

was only the beginning. You've unleashed something far more dangerous than you realize. The price of your sacrifice has only just begun."

The shadows closed in around them, and Lira's heart pounded as the creature lunged. She raised her sword, the blade glowing with the faint warmth of the fire that had once burned in her veins.

This was it—the final battle, the last stand. They had fought for the world, for a future free from the chains of winter. And now, they would fight to protect that future.

The fire and the ice were colliding, and Lira would not let the darkness win again.

Lira's sword hummed in the air as she swung it, the blade cutting through the tension in the ruins. The creature before her, a shadow of ice and ancient power, seemed to writhe with fury as she met its force, the magic that had bound it to this place now raging against her every move. The cold that surrounded her felt like a living thing, a suffocating weight pressing down on her shoulders, but she would not back down.

The figure, its form flickering like smoke, surged forward again, its shadowy tendrils reaching for her, sharp as daggers. Lira's heart pounded, every instinct urging her to fight, to protect everything they had fought for. She could feel the dark magic wrapping around her, trying to pull her into its grasp. But she had come too far to let it consume her now.

With a cry, she lunged forward, her sword slashing through the air, sending sparks of warmth crackling in the icy chill. The blade made contact with the shadowy creature, and it recoiled, howling in rage. The ground beneath them trembled, and the stone altar began to crack, as if the very structure of the ruins was responding to the chaos.

"You cannot defeat me," the creature hissed, its voice a low, icy whisper that sent shivers down Lira's spine. "You have already awoken what should have remained sealed. The price of your freedom will be paid with your souls."

Lira gritted her teeth, the weight of its words sinking into her chest. But there was no turning back. She could feel the land itself shifting, the magic in the ruins stirring in response to the battle. The relic had been destroyed, but the magic it had held— the cold, the darkness—was still anchored here. If she didn't destroy this creature, if she didn't sever the bond once and for all, everything they had fought for would be lost.

Eryn's voice broke through her thoughts, filled with urgency. "Lira! We need to stop it—*now*! We can't keep fighting like this."

Lira nodded, but she didn't take her eyes off the creature. She could feel the energy in the air, the pulse of ancient magic trying to drag her down, and she knew what she had to do. She had to reach deeper into herself than she ever had before, into the magic she had awakened with her sacrifice. But it came at a cost—a cost she wasn't sure she could afford.

"Eryn, I need you to trust me," Lira called over her shoulder, her voice steady despite the chaos.

"I trust you," he replied, his eyes filled with a mix of fear and determination. "I always will."

The creature howled again, the shadowy tendrils lashing out, but Lira didn't move. She closed her eyes, drawing in a deep breath. She could feel the magic inside her, still there, but unstable, flickering like a dying ember. But it was more than that now—she had come to understand it. The magic had never been just about control, just about the cold. It was life, too. It was creation and destruction, fire and ice, warmth and chill. It had the power to transform, but only if it was wielded with balance.

She reached out, feeling the power stir within her, calling it to the surface. But it wasn't just the relic's magic that responded—it was her own. The sacrifice she had made to end the curse, the part of herself she had given, had left her with an unfamiliar connection to the land, to the magic that pulsed in the very veins of Amara.

The ground beneath her feet rumbled as she gathered the magic, her hand stretching forward as she called upon it. Her pulse quickened, her heartbeat in time with the rhythm of the land itself. The creature roared in defiance, but Lira ignored it. She was no longer just a vessel for the magic. She had become a part of it.

In a flash, she released the power that had been building within her, the magic bursting from her hands in a wave of pure force. The air shimmered with energy, the chill of the creature's shadowy form warping, its body twisting in agony as the light and heat from Lira's magic clashed with its dark essence.

The creature screamed, a sound that rattled the very bones of the ruins, but it was too late. The blast of magic struck it directly, searing through the darkness, unraveling the ice and shadow that had once bound it. The ground beneath them cracked and splintered, the very foundations of the ancient ruins shaking as the last remnants of the creature's power were destroyed.

Lira fell to her knees, gasping for breath, the weight of the magic still coursing through her, pulling at her very soul. The world around her seemed to tilt, spinning, and she struggled to stay upright. Eryn was at her side in an instant, his hand steady on her shoulder, his eyes wide with concern.

"Lira, stay with me," he urged, his voice thick with emotion. "We did it. It's over."

But Lira could barely hear him over the ringing in her ears, the thrum of magic still pulsing through her. She had given everything—her strength, her life force—and now the price of that sacrifice was catching up to her.

The air around them grew still, and as the last remnants of the creature's shadow dissolved into the wind, the ruins began to settle. The land was no longer shaking, the tremors slowly fading as the last of the dark energy dissipated. Lira could feel the warmth of the sun growing stronger, the light that had once felt distant now reaching her with a renewed strength.

But she wasn't sure how much longer she could hold on.

"I'm sorry," she whispered, her voice ragged. "I didn't know what I was doing."

Eryn's hand tightened on her shoulder, his face filled with concern but also a deep understanding. "You did what needed to be done," he said quietly. "You gave everything, Lira. And we have a future because of it."

Lira closed her eyes, the exhaustion pulling her down. The cold still lingered, but it wasn't the same as before. The shadows had been pushed back, but the magic—the fire and ice—was still a part of her. And she wasn't sure how long it would remain under control.

She felt Eryn's arms around her, steadying her as her body swayed. "We'll find a way to make this right," he whispered. "You're not alone. We'll face whatever comes next. Together."

Lira clung to his words, to the warmth of his embrace, knowing that despite the sacrifice, despite the price they had paid, they had one another. Together, they had changed the world. But what would the future hold? What would the cost of this power be? The land had been freed, the curse shattered, but the magic was still here—deep within the earth, deep within her.

And as the last remnants of the cold began to recede, a new question loomed over them both: *What now?*

The battle was over, but the war—for their hearts, their souls, and the future of Amara—had only just begun.

The first light of dawn washed over the ruins, but in the distance, in the heart of the land that had been awakened, a new storm was brewing, and no one knew what would come next.

Sixteen

The War of the Seasons

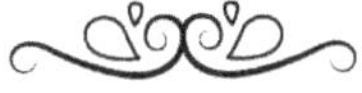

The winds had grown colder.

It had been months since Lira and Eryn had shattered the curse, months since the Queen's reign had crumbled beneath the weight of their sacrifice. The land had been slowly warming, the ice receding, the soil breathing once more. But now, the air felt heavy again, as if the very earth was holding its breath, waiting for the storm that was about to break.

The once-frozen rivers that now flowed freely had begun to churn with an ominous energy. The sun, once a promise of life, now felt like a distant memory, obscured by dark clouds that seemed to gather on the horizon. The first buds of spring, so brave just weeks ago, now struggled to thrive against the creeping cold that had returned, too soon, too fierce.

The land was shifting, and so were the people.

Lira stood at the edge of the camp, her back to the vast, empty wilderness, her eyes fixed on the distance. The tension in the air was palpable, a weight that clung to her skin like frost. The sounds of soldiers preparing for battle echoed around her—armor clattering, swords being sharpened, orders being shouted—but all of it felt distant, muffled by the fear that had taken root in her chest.

Behind her, Eryn's voice broke through the quiet. "Lira."

She turned to face him, her heart heavy with the same dread that had consumed her for days. Eryn's eyes, usually steady, now flickered with the same uncertainty that had been plaguing her. His jaw was clenched, his posture tense, but it was the tension in his eyes that troubled her most. They had fought together before, stood side by side in the face of impossible odds. But this—this war—felt different. The stakes were higher, and the price of failure felt too great.

"Eryn…" she started, her voice strained with the weight of the question she knew needed to be asked. "Do you think we're doing the right thing? Fighting this war… leading the charge against the very magic that has kept this land frozen for centuries?"

Eryn's gaze softened, and he stepped closer to her, his hand resting on her shoulder. His touch was grounding, but there was a weight in his eyes that she hadn't seen before. "I don't know if we're doing the right thing, Lira. I don't know if any of this makes sense anymore. But I know one thing—we can't let them bring the winter back. We can't let them take control of the magic we fought so hard to release."

Lira closed her eyes, feeling the sting of the cold on her skin. The chill in the air was no longer just a physical presence—it had become something deeper, something that crept into her soul. The forces that had once been under the Queen's control were now rallying to bring back the eternal winter. They sought the power of the magic that had once bound the land in ice, believing that only through the return of the old order could they restore the balance.

But the price of that power was too great. The cost of control was too high.

"There's so much at stake now," Lira murmured, her voice barely a whisper. "So many people who still don't understand the magic, who want to cling to the old ways. The ones who want to bring back the Queen's rule, the winter… They're not just fighting for control. They're fighting for a future they can't even see."

Eryn's grip tightened on her shoulder, and he turned her toward him. "And we're fighting for the future we believe in. For the future we've already started to build. We can't let them undo everything we've done, everything we've fought for."

Lira's heart surged with the certainty in his words, but it was tempered by the fear that still gnawed at her insides. The cold was creeping back into the land, and with it, the darkness. The war wasn't just about the magic anymore—it was about the very soul of the kingdom, about whether the land would remain free or fall back into the hands of those who wished to control it.

"We've already sacrificed so much," Lira whispered. "What if—what if it's not enough? What if we lose this war?"

Eryn's expression softened, and he cupped her face in his hands, pulling her gently toward him. His voice was fierce, filled with a quiet fire that burned in his eyes. "We won't lose, Lira. Not while we're together. Not while we still have each other."

Her heart swelled at his words, and for a moment, she

allowed herself to believe in them. To believe in the future they could still create. But the war was upon them now, and there was no turning back. The forces they were about to face were far stronger than anything they had encountered before. The old guard—those who sought to return to the eternal winter— were gathering in the mountains, their numbers swelling as they prepared for the final battle.

The war of the seasons had begun.

The battlefield was a strange place. It was not just a field of steel and blood—it was a place where the very air seemed to crackle with magic. The ground beneath their feet was uneven, the once-soft earth now hardened by the cold that had crept back into the land. The remnants of spring were fading, replaced by the icy grip of winter that seemed to stretch farther with every passing moment.

Lira stood in the center of the battlefield, her sword in hand, her heart pounding in her chest. The soldiers of the rebellion, the ones who had fought alongside them, now stood shoulder to shoulder with her, their faces grim, their eyes filled with the same resolve that had carried them through so much already. They had once believed that breaking the curse would bring peace, that the thaw would heal the land. But now, they were standing on the precipice of war—fighting to protect the very future they had worked so hard to build.

On the opposing side, the forces that wished to restore the old order stood in formation, their armor gleaming coldly in the light, their banners raised high. They had come from the deepest shadows of the kingdom, from the forgotten corners where the Queen's reign had once held sway. Their leader—an enigmatic figure who had called himself the Herald of Winter— stood at the front, his gaze fixed on the rebellion with a cold, calculating intensity.

The battlefield was quiet, too quiet, as both sides waited, poised for the first move.

Lira could feel the tension in the air, the weight of the moment pressing down on her. Her grip tightened around her sword, and she glanced to her side, meeting Eryn's eyes. He was beside her, as always, his presence a steady anchor in the chaos of the world around them.

"They're here," she said, her voice low. "The ones who want to bring back the Queen's reign. The ones who want the cold."

Eryn's expression was hard, his eyes narrowed as he surveyed the enemy lines. "They'll fight for it, Lira. They'll fight with everything they have. But so will we."

Lira nodded, her heart hammering in her chest. This was it. The war they had been fighting to avoid was now unavoidable. The world was divided, and the land itself seemed to hold its breath, waiting for the first blow to be struck.

The moment stretched on, each second an eternity. And then, with a single, sharp cry, the battle began.

The clash of steel on steel filled the air, the sound of swords and shields ringing out as the two armies collided. Lira was swept up in the tide of battle, her movements instinctive, her blade flashing in the dim light as she cut through the enemy lines. But it wasn't just the physical fight that consumed her—it was the magic that swirled in the air, the power of the seasons themselves clashing as the forces of winter fought against the warmth of the rebellion's hope.

The cold seemed to settle over everything, a palpable presence that pressed in on them. The rebels fought with all their strength, but the enemy was relentless, their numbers overwhelming. The Herald of Winter moved through the battlefield with unnatural grace, his every step sending waves of frost and shadow through the air.

Lira's heart pounded as she saw him—saw the figure who had rallied the forces of winter, who had awakened the cold that now threatened to consume them all. She could feel the power of his magic rippling through the air, and the realization hit her like a punch to the chest: the battle was not just against the enemy—it was against the very essence of winter itself.

"Eryn," Lira shouted, her voice rising above the din of battle. "We need to stop him. We need to break his hold on the magic."

Eryn nodded, his face grim. "I'll get to him. Keep the others safe."

With a final, lingering glance, Eryn disappeared into the chaos, his movements swift and deadly. Lira turned her attention back to the battlefield, her sword raised, her mind focused. She couldn't let the enemy gain ground. They had to fight back—had to push the darkness away. The warmth, the light they had fought for, was worth every sacrifice. It had to be.

The battle raged on, the world around her a blur of steel, magic, and blood. But in the heart of the chaos, Lira could feel it—the tipping point, the moment when everything would be decided.

And then, with a roar, the Herald of Winter appeared before her, his eyes cold, his form shrouded in the very essence of ice and shadow.

"You are too late," he sneered, his voice like the crackling of ice. "The magic of winter is eternal. You cannot fight what is destined to return."

Lira met his gaze, her sword steady in her grip. "We've already broken the curse. The world is changing, and you can't stop it."

The Herald laughed, the sound cruel and mocking. "You think you've won? You've only awakened the true power. You've only unleashed the storm."

And in that moment, Lira knew—this wasn't just a battle for control of the magic. This was a battle for the very soul of the kingdom.

With a cry, she launched herself at him, her sword raised high, the fire of her resolve burning as bright as the first light of dawn.

Lira's sword clashed against the Herald of Winter's staff, sending a jolt of icy energy up her arm. The cold that radiated from his staff felt as though it had frozen her very bones, but she didn't falter. She had fought too hard, sacrificed too much to let this figure of winter, of ancient darkness, have dominion over the land once more.

The Herald's eyes gleamed with the same chilling arrogance that had haunted the Queen's reign, but there was something more beneath that cold exterior—something ancient, something powerful. He stepped back, his movements fluid like the shifting of ice on a frozen lake, and he lifted his staff, summoning the air around them to freeze, the ground beneath her feet cracking with the sudden onslaught of frost.

"Your defiance is futile," he said, his voice deep and resonant, like the groaning of glaciers. "Winter is inevitable. It will return, no matter how you fight. It was never about the Queen's control, child. It is the nature of this world, the balance of fire and ice. You cannot change it."

Lira's heart raced, but her resolve hardened. "The world *can* change," she spat, her sword raised to meet his magic. "It's not the land that's broken. It's the way people choose to wield it. The choice was always theirs, and it will always be."

The Herald's lips curled into a wicked smile, his eyes flickering with something like disdain. He raised his staff high, and the frost around them intensified. Snow began to swirl, the air thickening with a biting cold that stung Lira's skin. Her breath formed icy clouds in the air, and she could feel the magic of the land itself pushing against her, trying to freeze her in place.

But she wasn't afraid. She had fought to change this world. She had fought for the warmth, for the fire that burned inside of her, that had come to represent the future she wanted to build.

"No, I won't let you," she whispered to herself, the words a fierce vow.

With a roar, she drove her sword downward, channeling the power within her, the magic she had unlocked in herself during the sacrifice to break the curse. The blade met the ground with a shockwave, and the earth trembled beneath her feet. The very ground seemed to react to the call of her magic, crackling with warmth and light. The frost that had started to swallow the air turned into steam, rising up in swirling clouds, as if retreating from the fire that now surged through her veins.

The Herald staggered back, his staff cracking against the growing heat. "Impossible..." he murmured, his voice shaking for the first time.

But Lira didn't relent. Her magic surged outward, growing with each beat of her heart. "The fire is as much a part of this world as the ice," she shouted, her sword glowing with the light of her conviction. "And we have the power to choose which one we wield."

With one final thrust, the sword connected with the Herald's staff, shattering the ice that had formed around it. The ground beneath them cracked, the earth shuddering as the power of her blow sent a wave of energy through the battlefield. The Herald staggered, his form wavering as though the very magic that sustained him was unraveling.

Lira's body burned with the magic, and for a moment, she thought she might lose control, but then she felt Eryn's presence beside her. His hand was on hers, grounding her, lending her his strength. He had always been her anchor, and now, in this final moment, they were united in their defiance against the darkness that sought to reclaim the land.

Together, they raised their swords. Together, they became a force of nature, a blaze that would burn away the shadows.

"You cannot undo the balance," the Herald sneered, his voice weak now, flickering as if his power was fading with each passing second. "Winter will come again. It always does."

"But not on your terms," Lira said, her voice steady, her heart full of fire. "The world will change, not because of fear, but because of choice."

She lunged forward, her sword cutting through the cold, and with one final strike, the Herald of Winter fell to his knees, his staff shattering into a thousand shards. The cold that had suffocated the land began to retreat, the last remnants of his shadowy form dissipating like fog in the morning sun.

The battlefield fell silent. The wind stopped howling. The crackling of magic faded into the distance.

For a moment, Lira could barely hear her own breathing, as though the world had come to a standstill. She felt the weight of the battle lift from her shoulders, but also the weight of the cost. There had been sacrifices—many of them. Lives had been lost, families torn apart. But she knew now, more than ever, that this was a war worth fighting.

Eryn stood beside her, his breath ragged but steady. His hand brushed against hers, and he turned to face her, his eyes filled with a mixture of relief and unspoken grief.

"We did it," he said, his voice hoarse.

Lira nodded, but it wasn't just victory she felt. It was the beginning of something new, something they hadn't yet understood. The magic of the land had been unlocked, and with it, the balance of fire and ice had been shattered. But that didn't mean they had won the final battle. The land was still fragile. The people still divided. The choice was theirs, and theirs alone, whether they would live in the light of spring or fall back into the grip of eternal winter.

"Not yet," Lira said, her voice soft but filled with resolve. "This isn't over. There's still work to be done."

Eryn's gaze darkened, and he stepped closer, his hand slipping into hers. "What do we do now?" he asked, his voice thick with the weight of the uncertainty that still hung in the air.

Lira met his gaze, her eyes fierce. "We rebuild. We heal the land. And we fight for the future we know is possible."

The winds shifted. The sun began to break through the clouds that had gathered overhead, casting a warm light over the battlefield. The fire and the ice had collided, but the land had not been consumed. Instead, it had been tempered—tested and forged in the heat of battle.

Lira took a deep breath, her sword still in her hand, her heart still pounding. She could feel the pulse of the land beneath her feet, and the promise of a future that lay ahead. There would be no easy path forward. There would be challenges, pain, and sacrifice still to come. But together—together with Eryn, with those who had fought for the future—they would make sure that the dawn would come, and that the seasons would turn in favor of life.

As the warmth spread across the land, Lira knew one thing above all else: *They had won the war of the seasons.* Now, they would rebuild, and this time, they would not let the darkness take root again.

The battle was over. But the fight for the future was just beginning.

Seventeen

The Last Embrace

The sky above was a blanket of heavy, swirling clouds, the air thick with the weight of an impending storm. It wasn't just the atmosphere that felt tense—it was the land itself. The world, which had begun to thaw, now seemed to freeze in anticipation. The earth quivered beneath their feet, as though it, too, was bracing for the final blow.

Lira stood at the edge of a ridge, gazing out over the valley below. The battlefield stretched out before her, the ground marred with the scars of past struggles. The land had been broken, rebuilt, and now it was to be tested again. The forces that had rallied against the magic of spring, against the breaking of the curse, were marching toward them, their ranks swelling with each passing day.

Behind her, Eryn stood silent, his presence a constant reassurance. But today, his usual steady demeanor was tinged with something she had not seen before—uncertainty, doubt.

He wasn't the man she had stood beside through all their trials. She could feel the crack in their bond, the tension that stretched between them, pulling taut with every passing moment.

"We've come so far," Lira said softly, her voice barely a whisper against the wind. Her fingers clenched around the hilt of her sword, feeling the cold steel beneath her fingertips, grounding her to the present. "And yet, it feels like we're on the brink of losing it all."

Eryn moved to stand beside her, his face illuminated by the dim light of the setting sun. His eyes searched the horizon, where the distant smoke of battle rose into the sky like a dark promise. "We've fought to bring peace," he said quietly, his voice thick with the weight of the words. "But peace is a fragile thing. It's always been. The magic we've unleashed, the world we've tried to create—it's all at risk. And we can't protect it, not completely, without facing the greatest challenge of all."

Lira turned to face him, her heart aching with the truth in his words. Their journey had been one of constant sacrifice, of giving more than they thought they had to give. And now, they were at the precipice of the final battle, the war that would decide not just the fate of their love but the fate of the entire world.

"What if we can't do it, Eryn?" she whispered, the doubt creeping into her voice despite her best efforts to remain strong. "What if we're not strong enough to save everything we've worked for?"

Eryn's gaze softened as he turned to face her fully, his hand reaching out to touch hers. His fingers brushed against hers, warm and solid. "Lira, we've always had each other. That's the strength we need. We've always fought side by side, no matter the odds. We will find a way."

But even as his words brought comfort, they felt hollow. The weight of the world, the responsibility that had fallen on their shoulders, was too much for two people to bear alone. The love they had for each other had carried them through so many trials, but now, it felt like it might tear them apart. The choice before them was one they couldn't avoid: the final sacrifice. To secure the future of Amara, one of them would have to give everything—more than just their life, more than just their magic. They would have to give up the very essence of what made them who they were.

The truth was simple, and yet, impossible.

They had already given too much. And now, they were being asked to give the one thing they couldn't afford to lose: each other.

"I don't know if I can do this without you," Lira said, her voice shaking with the truth of it. "I've fought with you, for you, through everything. But now… Now I don't know how to face this without losing you."

Eryn's hand tightened around hers, his thumb brushing over her knuckles as if trying to hold onto her. "You won't have to," he said softly. "We're not doing this alone. We're doing this together. We always have."

Lira closed her eyes, feeling the warmth of his hand seep into hers, but even that warmth felt fragile, fleeting. The love they shared was the only thing that had kept her going through the darkest moments of their journey, but now it seemed as though that love might be the very thing that would tear them apart.

The armies of the old order were gathering. The forces that sought to bring back the eternal winter, to control the magic of the land, were marching toward them. And at the heart of it all was a choice—a choice that would define the future of Amara.

Lira took a deep breath, trying to steady the trembling in her chest. The world was on the edge of a knife, and there was no way to turn back. The final battle would come soon, and when it did, they would have to face their greatest challenge: the war within themselves.

"We'll fight to the end," she said, her voice firm with resolve. "But I need to know that whatever happens, we will still have each other."

Eryn's eyes shone with a fire that mirrored her own, a promise of strength and love that no war could ever extinguish. "Always."

As the wind picked up around them, swirling the last remnants of winter in its wake, Lira knew that this moment would define them—not just as warriors, but as people, as lovers, as guardians of a future they had yet to build. The fate of Amara rested in their hands, but the cost would be greater than either of them could imagine.

The battle began at dawn.

The sky was painted in shades of crimson and gold, the sun rising slowly over the horizon like a harbinger of both hope and destruction. The air was thick with the scent of smoke and iron, the sounds of drums echoing through the land as the two armies prepared to clash.

Lira stood at the front of her forces, Eryn by her side, her sword gripped tightly in her hand. The tension in the air was unbearable, the weight of the moment pressing down on her chest. She had always been ready for battle, but this—this was different. This was the war that would decide everything. This was the moment when they would either break the old order or succumb to it.

"We fight for freedom," Eryn said, his voice steady and unwavering as he looked out over their forces. "We fight for the future."

Lira nodded, her heart swelling with pride for the people who stood beside her. They had fought for this moment, had bled for this moment. But it wasn't enough. They would need more than strength and courage. They would need everything they had, and even then, it might not be enough.

As the battle horns sounded, the first wave of enemies surged forward, their cries echoing across the field. The old guard had arrived, led by those who sought to return the winter to the world. Their army was vast, their numbers greater than Lira's forces, and they carried with them the weight of centuries of fear and control.

Lira's heart hammered in her chest as she raised her sword. The world was a blur of movement, of battle cries and clashing steel, but she was focused—laser-focused—on the enemy before her. This was the final stand. This was the moment they would either rise or fall.

The first clash of swords rang out, the sound deafening as steel met steel. Lira's movements were fluid, practiced, instinctive. She cut through the ranks, her blade flashing in the sunlight, the warmth of the fire she had unleashed flowing through her. But even as she fought, her thoughts were on Eryn—on the bond they shared, the love that had kept them alive through all the horrors they had faced. Would it be enough to hold them together when the cost of victory was too high?

The battle surged forward, each swing of her sword, each

strike against her enemies, pushing her closer to the point of no return. But it was the magic that she felt most acutely—the swirling force in the air, the crackling energy of both fire and ice. The land itself seemed to pulse with the battle, as if it were alive, as if it were watching them, waiting for the final moment when the scales would tip.

And then, through the chaos, she saw him.

The leader of the old guard, cloaked in shadows and ice, stood at the edge of the battlefield, his eyes burning with cold fury. The Herald of Winter had come to claim the land, to restore the eternal winter. And in that moment, Lira knew what she had to do.

Eryn appeared at her side, his sword raised high. "We end this," he said, his voice steady.

With a final, determined breath, Lira nodded. Together, they fought their way through the battlefield, cutting through the ranks of their enemies. The Herald of Winter was within their reach.

And as they approached him, Lira knew this would be the moment that would decide everything.

But the cost of victory—of breaking the curse—would not come without sacrifice. Would not come without a price.

As Lira's sword clashed against the Herald's, she felt the cold of his magic press against her skin, the weight of it pushing her to the edge. She couldn't do this alone. She couldn't bear the weight of the world without Eryn.

The battle within herself was just as fierce as the one around her.

The Herald of Winter's laugh echoed across the battlefield, a cold, biting sound that sent a chill down Lira's spine. His eyes gleamed with the kind of darkness that could swallow the world whole. With every step, the land seemed to grow colder, the wind picking up, swirling around them like a storm that had no end.

"You think you can stop me?" the Herald sneered, his staff raised high, the frosty aura around it crackling with malicious energy. "You, the girl who dared to break the curse? The one who thought she could undo what has been set in motion for centuries?"

Lira's chest tightened, her grip on her sword firm as she faced him, her every muscle taut with tension. "I didn't just break the curse," she said, her voice filled with unshakable resolve. "I freed the land. I freed Amara. And I will not let you bring back the endless winter."

The Herald's smirk faded, and in its place, there was only a cold fury. "Foolish girl," he hissed. "The winter was never meant to be broken. It is the balance of this world. It is the very heart of this land. And you—" He pointed his staff at her, his voice rising in anger. "—are nothing but a speck of flame that will be snuffed out by the cold of eternity."

Lira stepped forward, raising her sword high, her eyes locked onto the Herald. "We are not bound by the balance you speak of," she said fiercely, her voice unwavering. "We choose our path. We choose our future. And we will not go back to the darkness."

Eryn appeared at her side, his eyes filled with determination, his sword gleaming in the dying light of the battlefield. "Together," he said, his voice steady and full of strength. "We can end this. We fight for the world we have fought to create."

The ground beneath them seemed to rumble, the battle around them a blur as the two armies clashed. But in the eye of the storm, it was just Lira and Eryn standing side by side, facing the Herald of Winter.

The Herald snarled, lifting his staff high. The air around them grew frigid, and frost began to creep across the ground. With a roar, he slammed his staff into the earth, sending a wave of ice crashing toward them.

Lira's heart thundered in her chest, but she didn't hesitate. She moved with precision, her body flowing like water as she dodged the oncoming blast of ice. Her sword shimmered with the warmth she had unlocked in herself—the fire that had been ignited when she had made the ultimate sacrifice. That same fire surged through her, empowering her, making her feel invincible.

She struck with all her might, her blade cutting through the freezing air, slashing through the Herald's magic. But it wasn't enough. He was too powerful. The frost he controlled was ancient, too deeply rooted in the land.

Eryn was right beside her, fighting with the same passion, his strikes matching hers in perfect harmony. Together, they pressed forward, but the Herald's dark magic pushed back, encasing them in an impenetrable frost that chilled their very souls.

Lira's chest burned with the effort, but the cold was relentless, creeping into her bones. She could feel herself weakening, the energy that had carried her through so many battles starting to fade. The darkness was pushing in, trying to swallow the warmth she had fought so hard to build.

"Lira!" Eryn's voice cut through the ice, his hand reaching out to grab hers. "We need to fight this together. The land… the magic is still unstable. We can't fight him alone."

Lira turned to him, her heart aching with the truth in his

words. They had been bound together by more than just love—they had been bound by the magic that connected them, the land that had once been frozen and now began to thaw. But that connection, that magic, was fragile. They had broken the curse, but in doing so, they had awakened something ancient, something that had been waiting to return.

"We are together," she whispered, her fingers tightening around his hand. "But we need to finish what we started. We need to make sure the world we're fighting for is strong enough to survive."

They turned back toward the Herald, whose magic seemed to surge, becoming more violent with every passing second. His eyes burned with the power of the ancient winter, his staff crackling with raw, unbridled force. The land seemed to freeze under his command, the winds howling like wolves, the snow rising in towering columns around them.

"You cannot fight what has already been set in motion," the Herald spat, his voice rising with fury. "I am the embodiment of winter itself. You are nothing but fleeting sparks in the dark."

Lira's body burned with the fire of the magic she had unleashed, but the chill that surrounded her threatened to snuff it out. She could feel the cold inside of her, creeping deeper, pulling at her strength. But she wasn't going to let it win.

She glanced at Eryn, and he nodded, as if reading her thoughts. Together, they raised their swords, a single, unified force against the Herald's power. They could feel the energy shifting—their magic, their love, the land itself—working together to create something greater than either of them could alone.

Lira felt it first, a warm pulse deep within her, like the heartbeat of the land, like the sun breaking through the clouds after a long winter. It spread from her chest, out through her arms, down into the sword she held, into the very earth beneath her feet. It was the power of the fire and ice, the balance they had always sought but never fully understood until now.

And in that moment, everything came together. The warmth of spring, the fire of creation, and the cold of winter—together, they would forge a new world.

With a cry, Lira and Eryn struck forward, their swords gleaming with the combined power of their magic. The Herald's staff met their blades, but it was no match for the force that came from within them.

There was a moment of absolute stillness—an eternal silence—as the clash of magic filled the air with a bright, blinding light.

Then, with a deafening crack, the Herald's staff shattered. The blast of energy that erupted from the collision was enough to send shockwaves through the battlefield, knocking both armies off their feet. The cold that had clung to the land for so long began to dissipate, replaced by a warmth that spread like a wildfire, consuming everything in its path.

Lira's legs gave out beneath her as the force of the magic sent her tumbling to the ground. Eryn caught her in his arms, his eyes wide with concern. "Lira? Lira, are you okay?"

Her breath was shallow, her body trembling with the aftershocks of the magic that had coursed through her, but the warmth, the fire, was still inside her. She had won. They had won.

"I'm here," she whispered, her voice hoarse. "We did it. It's over."

The battle raged on around them, but the war had ended. The cold was gone. The Herald was vanquished. The magic had been balanced. The curse had been broken for good.

But as she lay there in Eryn's arms, the weight of the sacrifice—the cost of what they had done—settled on her heart like a stone. They had won, yes, but at what cost? The world had been saved, but the land, the people, had been through so much. They would rebuild, yes. But the question remained: would the magic they had unlocked be enough to sustain the world, or would it break under the weight of their choices?

Lira didn't have the answer. All she knew was that she had done everything she could. She had given everything to ensure the future of the land she loved. And now, in the stillness that followed, she allowed herself to rest—her body in Eryn's arms, her heart still beating in time with his.

For the first time in a long while, the battle was over. And the world was theirs to shape, together.

Eighteen

The Dawn of Spring

The first rays of sunlight sliced through the thick clouds, bathing the land in a soft, golden glow. It was a light that felt both fragile and eternal, as though the world was waking from a long, endless sleep. Lira stood at the edge of the hill, her gaze fixed on the horizon where the dark remnants of winter were finally beginning to fade. The trees that had once stood bare, their branches twisted and stark against the sky, now stirred with the first signs of life. Buds appeared on the limbs, fragile at first but filled with the promise of rebirth. The wind, once sharp with cold, had softened to a gentle breeze, carrying with it the scent of earth and new growth.

But as she stood there, the wind tugging at her cloak, Lira knew that the land would never truly be the same again.

"Lira," Eryn's voice broke through her thoughts. She turned to see him approaching, his face as serious as always, though his eyes held something softer now—a warmth that she hadn't seen in him before. She couldn't help but smile at the sight of him, the man who had stood by her side through every storm, through every battle.

"Eryn," she greeted him, her voice quiet, yet carrying an unspoken weight. "It's over. The winter… the cold—it's gone."

Eryn stood next to her, his hand brushing against hers, a silent comfort in the stillness between them. "It is. But the land…" His voice trailed off, as if searching for the right words. "The land still needs us, Lira. It still needs our strength."

Lira nodded. She had been thinking the same thing. The war, the battle they had fought to break the curse, was over—but the true work had only just begun. The peace they had won was fragile, like the first blossom of spring. There was so much left to rebuild, so much to restore. The people of Amara were no longer bound by the chains of eternal winter, but they were still lost, still scarred by the years of fear, suffering, and oppression.

The memories of the past couldn't be easily erased.

"Do you think they'll ever be able to trust again?" Lira asked, her voice low as she watched the land unfold before her. The rolling hills, the valleys that had once been buried in snow, now looked like something out of a dream. A world reborn. But that rebirth was incomplete. The people needed to heal. They needed hope.

Eryn took a deep breath, his fingers brushing against hers. "They will," he said with quiet certainty. "In time, they'll see that the land is not the enemy anymore. Winter is gone. But so is the Queen. The old ways—those are the real enemies now. They're the ones that want to keep this land in darkness. And it's up to us to make sure that doesn't happen."

Lira looked at him, her heart swelling with love for the man who had become her anchor in a world that had been upturned by chaos. His eyes were filled with the same determination that had driven them both through the darkest hours. He wasn't just fighting for Amara anymore. He was fighting for the future, for the love they shared, and for the world they would build together.

"I don't know what the future holds," Lira said softly. "But I know that as long as we're together, we can face it."

Eryn smiled, the warmth in his expression reaching his eyes, and took her hand fully in his. "That's all that matters. We've come this far together. And we'll keep going, no matter what."

The wind stirred around them, carrying with it the sounds of birds singing in the trees, the hum of life returning to the world they had saved. They stood there for a long moment, side by side, the weight of their journey settling over them like a soft, heavy blanket. They had lost so much to get to this point. So many sacrifices. So many moments where it had felt like there was no way forward.

But now, there was light.

The weeks that followed were both a blur and an eternity. The armies that had once fought against them were now a distant memory, scattered, disbanded, their leaders either vanquished or fled. The Queen's legacy had crumbled into dust, and with it, the cold grip of winter. But that didn't mean the world was free from its scars.

Lira and Eryn, together, led the rebuilding effort. They traveled from village to village, city to city, meeting with the people, offering them the hope that they could still have a future. The first signs of spring were everywhere, but it wasn't enough to erase the suffering of the past. The people had lived so long in fear, so long under the cold hand of tyranny, that they didn't know how to trust the warmth that was now spreading across the land.

There was work to be done. There were wounds to heal.

They returned to the capital, to the heart of the kingdom, where the remnants of the old world still lingered like shadows in the corners of the streets. The palace stood as a silent monument to the past, a cold, imposing structure that had once been a symbol of power. Now, it seemed out of place in the light of the new world.

Lira stood at the foot of the steps leading up to the grand entrance, her heart heavy as she looked at the once-majestic building. The memories of the battles, the pain, the sacrifices, all seemed to press down on her. But at the same time, there was something new in the air. Something that told her that this place—this kingdom—could be something better.

"We have to make sure they know the truth," Eryn said, his voice steady as he stood beside her, his hand resting on her shoulder. "We have to make sure they understand that the past is over."

Lira turned to him, meeting his gaze. "They will," she said softly. "But it's going to take time. The peace we've fought for... it's fragile. They have to see it with their own eyes."

They walked up the steps, their steps echoing in the silence. The palace doors were wide open, welcoming them into the heart of the kingdom they had fought so hard to save. Inside, the once grand hallways were now filled with the sound of bustling workers and the hum of people who had come to rebuild, to reclaim what had been lost.

As they entered the grand hall, Lira felt the weight of what they had done. She and Eryn had broken the curse, had freed the land, but they were not done yet. The world needed more than just their love—it needed their leadership, their wisdom, and their strength. They had to be the foundation on which this new world would be built.

Lira felt Eryn's presence beside her, solid and unwavering. Together, they had faced down the darkness. Together, they had fought for their future. And together, they would ensure that the warmth of spring—of new beginnings—would not fade.

Days turned into weeks, and weeks into months. The world slowly began to heal. The people of Amara, scarred by years of cold and fear, slowly began to rebuild their homes, their cities, their lives. There were challenges—factions who still clung to the old ways, whispers of rebellion that threatened to undo the peace they had fought for—but Lira and Eryn faced them together, side by side.

Their love had become the rallying cry for the future. It was no longer just a personal bond. It was a symbol of hope, a reminder that even in the darkest of times, love could be the thing that saved the world.

They built a kingdom of warmth, of light, of balance—one where the magic of fire and ice would no longer be controlled by fear. They built a kingdom that would stand as a testament to the power of choice, of change, and of sacrifice.

And as the seasons turned, and the land continued to bloom and grow, Lira knew that the dawn of spring wasn't just a season. It was a new beginning—a new age. An age they had fought for, bled for, and finally, at long last, claimed.

The cost had been great, but the future—so full of promise—was worth it. As she stood with Eryn by her side, watching the sun dip below the horizon, she knew that this was just the beginning. Together, they would face whatever came next, for they had already proven that no darkness could stand against the light of their love. And no winter could hold sway over a world that had chosen to embrace the warmth of spring.

The war was over.

The dawn had come.

And with it, a new world had been born.

The air was thick with the promise of the future as Lira and Eryn stood side by side, gazing over the kingdom they had helped rebuild. The sun had dipped below the horizon, but the soft afterglow still clung to the earth like a fading memory of the warmth that had begun to settle into the land. The world felt full of potential, the weight of the past melting away like snow in the spring.

But even in this moment of peace, there was an undeniable undercurrent of tension. The world was healing, yes—but it was not yet whole. There were too many pieces that had been broken over the years, too many people who had suffered in silence, too many who still clung to the old ways out of fear, out of habit. Change was inevitable, but it was never easy. And Lira could feel the weight of that truth pressing on her shoulders, as much as the warmth of the sun on her face.

Beside her, Eryn stood tall, his posture strong yet tempered with the same quiet awareness that had guided them through the darkest of times. He was her rock, the constant through every storm. But Lira could sense the unease in him too— his thoughts, his heart, as conflicted as hers. They had saved the world. They had broken the curse, defeated the Herald of Winter, and won the peace they had longed for. But there was still something missing. There was still the question of what came next.

"I never thought this day would come," Lira said softly, her voice barely above a whisper, but it carried the weight of all the years they had fought, all the battles they had endured.

Eryn turned to her, his eyes meeting hers, a soft smile tugging at his lips. "I don't think any of us did," he replied, his voice tinged with quiet wonder. "But here we are. After everything."

Lira's gaze drifted over the landscape. The fields that had once been barren were now alive with green. The trees, once skeletal, now stood tall and proud, their branches laden with fresh leaves. The rivers, which had been locked in ice for so long, flowed with fresh, clear water. The land had responded to the thaw, and so too had the people. They were rebuilding, starting anew. But the scars of the past still lingered in their eyes. The cold had left them with more than just a broken kingdom—it had left them with broken hearts.

Eryn took her hand, the simple touch grounding her as they both stood in silence, watching the last traces of daylight fade. His touch, his presence, was the one thing that had always kept her going, even in the darkest hours. And now, as they faced the uncertainty of a future filled with rebuilding and healing, it was that same bond that kept her steady.

"I don't know if I can do this without you," Lira murmured, her voice filled with a quiet ache. "This... this responsibility. I'm not sure I'm strong enough to carry it."

Eryn turned fully to face her, his expression softening with understanding. His hand cupped her cheek, the warmth of his touch chasing away the last of the shadows in her heart. "You don't have to do it alone. We're in this together, Lira. We always have been."

The weight of his words settled over her, but it didn't fully dispel the uncertainty she felt. The kingdom was theirs to rebuild, yes—but they were more than just rulers now. They were the symbol of hope for the future, the beacon of everything that had been fought for. Their love, their bond, had become the foundation on which this new world would be built. And yet, the enormity of that task made her heart heavy.

"Do you ever wonder if we've done the right thing?" Lira asked, her voice almost a whisper, as though afraid to speak the question aloud. "The cost of everything we've done—how much of us have we sacrificed, Eryn? Is it enough?"

Eryn's eyes softened with something akin to sorrow, but also understanding. "I think about it every day," he admitted. "We've fought for something more than ourselves. More than our love. We've fought for a future. But even now, I can't say what that future will look like. I don't know what the world will become, what will happen to the people we've saved. But what I do know is that we're still standing. We're still here, together. And that's worth something."

Lira's heart tightened in her chest as she looked into his eyes. She could see the same uncertainty in him, the same battle within. They had faced wars of steel and magic, battles of life and death, but this—the rebuilding, the healing—was something entirely different. They were building something that could never be undone. Something they had to protect, not with swords or magic, but with love, patience, and the wisdom they had gained through sacrifice.

"I'm scared, Eryn," she confessed, her voice breaking slightly. "I'm scared that we've done too much. That we've changed the world in ways we can't control."

Eryn pulled her into his arms, holding her close as the weight of her words settled between them. He didn't speak at first, just let the silence stretch between them, heavy with the unspoken truths that hung in the air.

"We've already given everything to make this world better," he said softly. "And we will continue to give. But that doesn't mean we're alone in this. The people of Amara—they will help us rebuild. They will stand with us. The love we share isn't just between us anymore. It's a bond that connects us all. And that's what will make this new world stronger."

Lira closed her eyes, letting herself rest against him for a moment. His words, simple but profound, settled in her chest, bringing a sense of calm she hadn't realized she'd been missing. Maybe they had done everything they could. Maybe they had given all they had to this land, to the people they had fought for.

And yet, the question remained: *Was it enough?*

A distant sound, faint at first but growing louder, reached her ears. The murmur of voices. The footsteps of soldiers and workers, the hum of activity filling the air as the kingdom, slowly but surely, came back to life. Lira lifted her head from Eryn's chest, her eyes scanning the horizon once more. She could see the people gathered, working in unison. They were clearing the old streets, rebuilding homes, planting new crops. Life, once more, was stirring in every corner of the kingdom.

"Maybe," Lira said softly, her voice full of conviction, "maybe it's not about being perfect. Maybe it's about trying. Trying to make it right. Trying to keep the fire alive."

Eryn looked at her, his expression soft, his hand brushing a lock of hair from her face. "You've always known that," he said with a smile that warmed her heart. "And you've always been stronger than you think."

Lira smiled back, though it was a smile tinged with sadness. They had done so much, and yet there was still so much left to do. The world was healing, but it was fragile. She could feel it in her bones—the land, the people—everything was still raw, still broken in some ways. The magic that had been unleashed, the love they had fought for, was all they had to rebuild with.

The morning stretched on, the sun climbing higher in the sky, the warmth spreading across the land. It felt like a promise. A new beginning.

"We'll face it together," Eryn said, his voice steady. "All of it. No matter what."

Lira nodded, squeezing his hand tightly. They had come so far, and there was still a long road ahead of them. But now, standing on the threshold of a new world, she knew that they would walk that road together.

Together, they had fought for the dawn.

And now, together, they would build the world that dawn would bring.

As the weeks passed, the healing continued. The land flourished under the warmth of spring, the first true spring in centuries. The people of Amara, scarred by their past, began to rebuild not just their homes but their hearts. They trusted again. Slowly, but surely, they learned to trust in the love and sacrifice that had saved them.

And in that quiet, golden light, Lira and Eryn found their place. Their love, once a flickering flame in the darkness, became the foundation on which this new world stood. With every brick laid, with every seed planted, they built a future. And though the challenges ahead were uncertain, one thing was sure: they would face them together.

Nineteen

The Return of the Moon

The moon hung high above, its light piercing through the canopy of trees that stretched across the horizon. It bathed the land in a silver glow, turning the once barren fields into shimmering pools of light. The night had come to Amara, but it was a night like no other—one that had not been seen in centuries. The full moon, bright and unyielding, was a reminder of all they had fought for. A symbol of the land's rebirth, of the sacrifices made and the love that had not only survived the trials of war but had thrived.

Lira stood at the edge of the cliff, her silhouette outlined against the vast sky, her gaze fixed on the moon as it hung in the heavens like a silent witness to their struggles. It had been years since the battle, since the cold had finally retreated, and the world had begun its slow but steady recovery. And yet, on nights like this, when the air was still and the stars seemed to pulse with life, she could still feel the weight of those long years pressing against her chest.

Eryn was beside her, his presence as constant and grounding as it had always been. He stood tall, his hand resting lightly on the hilt of his sword, but his eyes, like hers, were drawn to the moon. There was something sacred in its glow tonight. Something that spoke of all they had done, all they had endured. And though the world had changed, and peace had been restored, it was the memory of those dark days, of the battles fought and won, that seemed to burn brightest now, like a fire that could never be extinguished.

Lira turned to him, the faintest of smiles tugging at her lips. "Do you ever wonder if we truly understand the depth of what we've done?"

Eryn's expression softened, his eyes meeting hers. "We may never fully understand it, Lira. What we did wasn't just about breaking a curse or defeating the Herald. It was about giving the people of Amara the chance to choose their future. To live in the warmth of a world free from fear. And that, I think, is something that will always remain."

Lira's heart swelled at his words, but there was a quiet sadness that lingered within her. Over the years, they had rebuilt the land. They had restored Amara, piece by piece, and helped the people who had once lived in the shadows of the Queen's rule find their footing in the new world. But the war, the sacrifices, the long years of struggle—it all seemed to linger beneath the surface, like a faint echo of the past that never truly faded.

"I wonder if we were ever meant to be part of this world," she whispered, her voice carrying the weight of her unspoken thoughts. "To be the ones to change it."

Eryn took a step closer to her, his hand brushing against

hers. "We were meant to do this, Lira. We were always meant to lead, to fight for what we believed in. The love we share… it was the fire that burned through the darkness. It will always burn, even when the shadows of the past try to creep back in."

Lira's eyes glistened as she looked at him, her chest tightening with a mixture of pride and sorrow. They had fought for each other, for the world, for the love that had brought them together. But there had been a cost—a cost they would carry with them for the rest of their lives.

The moonlight seemed to grow brighter as she took a deep breath, letting the cool night air fill her lungs. The world had healed, yes, but the scars were still there. And even though the kingdom was thriving, the memories of what had been lost, of what they had sacrificed, could never be erased.

"Sometimes, I feel as though the world we've built is still fragile," Lira said softly. "Like it could slip through our fingers if we're not careful."

Eryn nodded, his eyes reflecting the same understanding. "The world is always fragile, Lira. It's the nature of things. But we've built it on a foundation stronger than any curse, stronger than any darkness. Our love… the legacy of everything we've fought for… it's something that will live on, even when we're gone."

Lira turned away from the cliff, her gaze falling to the valley below. The villages, the fields, the homes—all of them thriving under the warmth of spring. The land, once locked in ice and shadow, was now alive with the sounds of people laughing, working, living. It was a world they had dreamed of, a world they had fought for. But she knew that it was a fragile thing, one that needed constant care.

"We built this," she said quietly, "but it's up to them now. The people of Amara. They must carry the flame forward."

Eryn stepped beside her, his presence a steady comfort. "And they will," he said, his voice filled with quiet certainty. "Because the love you and I share, Lira, is something that will never fade. It is the foundation on which this world will stand. It is the fire that will always light their way."

The wind stirred around them, carrying with it the scent of fresh earth and blooming flowers. It was a world reborn, but the memory of the struggle, the cost of peace, would always remain in their hearts.

Lira looked up at the moon once more, her gaze lingering on its soft, glowing light. It was a symbol—one that had witnessed their every battle, their every sacrifice. And now, it seemed to shine brighter than ever, as if it, too, was celebrating the victory they had achieved together.

The moon, once a silent witness to their struggles, now seemed to whisper of the love that had defied the harshest winters, of the bond that had held them together when everything else had seemed lost. It was a symbol of hope, of resilience, of a love that would never be broken.

"It's strange," Lira murmured, "to think that this is how it ends. That the battle is over, that the curse is truly gone. All we have left is this world we've made, this life we've fought for."

Eryn's hand found hers again, and this time, he pulled her closer, wrapping his arms around her. "It's not over," he said softly, his voice filled with quiet conviction. "The fight may be over, but the journey is just beginning. There will be challenges ahead, yes. There will be hardships, times when it feels like the world is slipping through our fingers. But as long as we have each other, as long as we hold on to what we've built, we will always find our way."

Lira closed her eyes, leaning against him as the weight of his words settled in her chest. She had given everything to this world, and now, in this quiet moment, she realized that the true gift had been the love they shared, the love that had carried them through the darkest of times. And now, that love would be the light that guided them forward.

"We will always have each other," she whispered, her voice steady. "And we will always have this world, this legacy. No matter what."

The moon above seemed to shine brighter in response, its light bathing the land in a soft, ethereal glow. It was a light that would never fade. It was a light that would guide them, and the world they had saved, for as long as the stars continued to shine in the sky.

As the night stretched on, Lira and Eryn stood together, hand in hand, watching the world below. The moon, the land, the people—they were all connected now, bound by the love that had been forged in the fires of sacrifice and strength. And no matter what challenges the future held, Lira knew one thing for certain: the love that had saved Amara would never be extinguished. It would live on, a beacon of hope, a symbol of all they had overcome, and all they had built.

The dawn of spring had come. And with it, the promise of a future full of life, love, and endless possibility. The moon, once a silent witness to their struggles, now stood as a testament to everything they had fought for—everything they had achieved. And as Lira looked up at the sky, she knew that the story of Amara was far from over. It was just beginning.

Together, they would face whatever came next, just as they had faced every challenge before. And the legacy of their love, like the light of the moon, would shine for all time.

Lira's gaze lingered on the moon, its silver light cascading down onto the earth below, washing the land in a glow that seemed to shimmer with the promise of more. The past, the pain, the loss—everything seemed so distant now, but the memories would never fade. It had been a long road to get here, and even now, standing in the silence of the night, she could feel the echoes of those struggles beneath the surface, a gentle reminder that nothing truly disappears.

Yet, somehow, the land felt at peace for the first time. The air was warmer, the earth richer, and the songs of life—the sounds of people, of animals, of a world awakening—had become a symphony, their notes filling the space where the cold had once silenced all.

Beside her, Eryn's warmth radiated, a steady presence in a world that had found its footing again. His hand found hers, and his thumb brushed over her knuckles in a familiar, comforting motion that always seemed to steady her heart.

"We've rebuilt so much," she said, her voice almost a whisper. It felt fragile, like the moon's glow might shatter the moment she spoke louder. "But I'm still afraid that it won't last. That the world might slip back into the shadows we fought to escape."

Eryn turned to face her, his eyes soft yet filled with the strength of someone who had endured the harshest winters, both literal and emotional. "It's normal to be afraid," he said, his voice calm, steady. "The world we built isn't perfect. It's fragile. But we're stronger now, Lira. We know how to fight for it. We know how to hold on to what matters. And we'll keep fighting—for ourselves, for the world, for the people."

His words wrapped around her like a blanket, warming the

doubt that had begun to creep into her heart. She had feared the future for so long. It had been a constant companion ever since the curse had been broken—always looming, always threatening. But in Eryn's arms, with the world stretching out before her, a new kind of hope blossomed, one she hadn't allowed herself to feel in years.

"We've built something," Lira said, finally turning away from the moon and meeting his eyes. "A world where people can finally choose. Where they can decide for themselves. But it's not just about what we've created. It's about how we hold on to it."

Eryn nodded, a small, understanding smile tugging at his lips. "It's never been about the battles we've fought, or the victory we won. It's about the choices we make now, every single day. We can't control everything. We can't predict what's coming. But as long as we face it together, we'll be okay."

Lira's heart skipped a beat as she held his gaze, feeling the weight of his words sink into her soul. For so long, she had fought to survive. She had fought to save the world, to break the curse that had bound them all in the frozen grip of eternal winter. And now, standing with Eryn, with the land healed and the future wide open, she realized the real battle had always been about love. About holding on to it when everything else seemed so fragile.

She took a deep breath, the cool night air filling her lungs. "Together," she echoed, her voice stronger now, filled with certainty.

A distant sound reached her ears—distant at first, but growing louder. The rustling of leaves, the hum of voices carried on the wind. The sounds of the world beginning to stir, to return to life.

"Do you hear that?" Lira asked, her eyes turning toward the trees.

Eryn listened, his expression shifting to one of focus. He nodded slowly. "The people. They've come."

Lira turned her attention back to the valley below, where the distant glow of lanterns flickered against the dark horizon. The first true signs of the people coming together, of gathering to celebrate the return of spring and the new world they had built. For so long, they had been fractured, divided by fear and the cold that had suffocated their world. Now, they were beginning to find their way again.

Eryn squeezed her hand. "They're waiting for us."

And just like that, the weight of the world seemed to shift again. Their fight wasn't over. The land had healed, yes, but so much more needed to be done. The people still needed guidance, still needed hope. And there, in the soft glow of the moon, Lira realized that their journey was only just beginning.

Together, they walked down the hill, hand in hand, toward the growing gathering below. The celebration would be a symbol—of the life that had been reclaimed, of the love that had led them through the darkest days. And as they reached the base of the hill, the sounds of music and laughter grew louder, the people who had once been bound by fear now standing side by side, united in the promise of the future.

The crowd was gathered near the center of the village, a massive bonfire roaring in the center, its light dancing across the faces of the people who had once been divided, who had once feared the very change they had fought for. But now, as the fire crackled and the moon above bathed them all in silver light, there was only unity. The people had come together to celebrate, to honor the sacrifices that had been made to bring them here.

Lira and Eryn stood at the edge of the crowd, watching as the people sang and danced, their voices echoing into the night sky. It felt like a dream, a reality that had seemed so distant not long ago. But now, here they were, living it—surrounded by the very people they had fought to free.

Eryn turned to her, his eyes shining with an intensity that made her heart race. "This is the world we fought for, Lira," he said softly. "This is what we've built."

Lira looked out over the crowd, her heart swelling with a pride she had never known. For all the battles they had fought, for all the sacrifices that had been made, this moment—this peace—was the reward. It wasn't just about survival. It was about living. About loving. About choosing to walk forward, side by side, into the future they had created.

"It's beautiful," she whispered, her voice filled with awe. "It's everything we dreamed of."

Eryn's hand tightened around hers, and he pulled her closer, his forehead resting gently against hers. "And it's just the beginning."

Lira's breath caught in her chest, the gravity of his words settling over her like a warm embrace. Yes, it was the beginning. They had only just begun to rebuild the world. There would be challenges, yes. There would be moments when doubt crept in, when the shadows of the past threatened to return. But together, they could face anything.

The moon above them seemed to pulse with an energy of its own, casting its light on the faces of the people who stood around them, celebrating the world they had fought to save. Its glow was a reminder of everything they had endured, everything they had sacrificed, and everything they had won.

And as it illuminated the land they had freed, Lira knew that their love, like the moon, would shine for all time.

For a long time, they stood together, watching the people celebrate their newfound peace. And in that quiet, unspoken moment, Lira and Eryn realized that the true legacy of their love was not just the world they had saved, but the future they had promised to build—a future where love, sacrifice, and hope would always lead the way.

And as the fire burned bright, and the moon looked down upon them all, Lira knew that no matter what came next, they would face it together. Their love was the light that had freed the land, and it would be the light that guided them into the dawn of a new age.

The night was still, the stars shining bright, and the land was alive with the promise of a future built on sacrifice, strength, and love.

And that future had only just begun.

Twenty

The Last Winter's Embrace

The wind howled across the vast expanse of the frozen mountains, its icy fingers clawing at the rocks, sending dust and snow swirling through the air. Below, the remnants of a once mighty fortress lay in ruins, its jagged spires rising from the broken stone like the remains of a long-dead beast. The land around it was cold and empty, devoid of life, yet alive with echoes of the past—echoes that threatened to swallow everything that had been built.

Lira stood at the edge of the cliff, her breath visible in the air, her cloak wrapped tightly around her, but the chill still gnawed at her bones. She had never fully been able to shake the feeling that something still lingered, something that would never fully release its grip on her heart. Though the winter had ended, there was something about the mountains, about this place, that reminded her of the cold that had once defined their world. Something that would never be truly erased.

Beside her, Eryn's presence was a constant warmth. His hand, strong and steady, brushed against hers, the connection between them still unshakable despite the time that had passed. The battles, the struggles, the pain—they had become memories, fading like smoke in the wind, but the bond between them? It was the one thing that had never wavered. And it would be the one thing that carried them forward into whatever lay ahead.

"Do you feel it too?" Lira's voice was barely a whisper, the words lost in the wind. "The cold."

Eryn's eyes softened as he looked out over the mountains, his gaze distant, contemplative. "I do," he said quietly. "But not the same way. Not like before. This is different. This is the reminder of what we overcame. The last remnants of a curse that sought to break us."

Lira nodded, her fingers curling into her palms as if she could hold onto the warmth of their shared strength. "I thought once the curse was broken, once the winter was gone, the land would finally be free. But this… this is the last piece of it, isn't it? The cold that will always remain, like a shadow."

Eryn stood taller, the cold wind brushing against his face, but his eyes never leaving her. "The world isn't just defined by what was. It's defined by what we choose to make of it now. And we've chosen to fight for warmth, for love, for a future."

"But there's always a price," Lira said, her gaze flickering to the distant horizon. "The magic we used—the lives we sacrificed—the cost of what we did is always present. The cold may be gone, but I can't shake the feeling that there's something still unfinished, something I haven't given up yet. Maybe the love we fought for isn't enough."

"Maybe," Eryn said, stepping closer, the warmth of his body

a shield against the cold that clung to her. "But we've already made the greatest sacrifice. The future we fought for, the peace we've built, is worth everything we've given. Love—true love—is never easy. It's always a challenge, always a fight. But in the end, it's the one thing that can carry us through, that will always endure, even when everything else falters."

The ground beneath their feet trembled slightly, a low rumble like distant thunder, but Lira's heart stilled. She could feel it in the air, the presence of something dark and ancient, something that still haunted these lands. She had believed that the battle was over, that the legacy of their struggle had been sealed. But now, in the stillness of this frozen place, she realized that they had not yet seen the full cost of their victory.

The wind shifted, carrying with it a sound—faint at first, like the whisper of a faraway voice. It grew louder, louder still, until it became unmistakable. The sound of ice cracking, of something deep beneath the earth awakening, stirring after centuries of dormancy. And then, she saw it.

A figure, emerging from the shadowed depths of the mountain pass. A silhouette, tall and regal, draped in flowing robes of ice and shadow. The figure stepped into the moonlight, revealing a face both familiar and unfamiliar. It was as though the winter itself had come alive, taking shape in the form of a figure from Lira's past—one she had thought long buried.

"Ysra?" Lira's voice broke the silence, her heart racing as she stared at the figure before her. The once-feared Queen, whose icy grip had held Amara for so long, stood before her, but she was not the same as she had once been. The woman who had ruled the land with an iron fist was now a shadow of the past, the coldness that had defined her still present, but in a form that seemed almost… fractured.

Ysra's eyes, once filled with venom and hatred, now gleamed with something different. It was as if she had been reborn, but not in a way that Lira could understand. The woman before her was not the tyrant she had once known, but neither was she the ally they had fought to become.

"You thought the curse was broken," Ysra said, her voice a soft hiss that carried through the air. "You thought the winter was gone. But the land is not so easily freed. You cannot undo what was written in the bones of the earth."

Eryn stepped in front of Lira, his stance protective. "You're wrong, Ysra," he said, his voice hard, unwavering. "We did break the curse. We freed the land. The magic of winter no longer rules here."

Ysra's lips curled into a smile, but it was not one of victory. It was a smile born of something darker, something older. "You freed the land from my grip, yes. But you did not free it from the magic that had been woven into it for centuries. The winter was not just a curse—it was a choice. A choice made to protect this world from something far worse."

Lira felt a chill creep down her spine, something that had nothing to do with the air around them, and everything to do with the truth in Ysra's words. "What do you mean?" she asked, her voice barely a whisper.

Ysra's eyes gleamed with something unsettling, something ancient. "I was never the true ruler of winter," she said. "I was merely its guardian. The winter was bound to this land as a defense—a defense against something far darker, something that would have consumed everything. You may have broken the curse, but you've opened the door to something far worse. And now, I have come to reclaim my role."

Lira's heart raced as the implications of Ysra's words sank

in. They had thought the battle was over, that the world was free. But in breaking the curse, in freeing the land from the eternal winter, they had unwittingly broken the last barrier between the world and the darkness that had once threatened to consume it.

The ground beneath their feet rumbled again, this time louder, more insistent. The mountains groaned as if they were coming to life, the air thick with an energy that felt ancient, predatory. Lira's mind raced, her thoughts spinning in a whirlwind of uncertainty. They had fought for so long, had sacrificed so much, only to find that the true enemy—one they hadn't even known existed—was still out there, waiting to reclaim the power that had been lost.

Eryn's voice broke through her thoughts, filled with determination. "We won't let you do this," he said, his hand gripping his sword, his eyes locked on Ysra with a fury that matched her own.

Ysra raised her hands, her fingers crackling with ice, the magic swirling around her like a storm. "You don't understand," she said, her voice low, dangerous. "This world was never meant to be free. The winter—the cold—it is the only thing that keeps the true darkness at bay. Without it, there is nothing stopping it from returning. And once it does, there will be no warmth left. No hope."

Lira felt a sudden surge of fear, but she pushed it down. They had come so far. They had fought so hard. She couldn't let it all slip away now.

"We'll fight," she said, her voice firm, her sword raised in front of her, the magic within her flaring. "We won't let you bring back the darkness."

Ysra's eyes darkened, her lips curling into a bitter smile. "You have no choice," she whispered. "The winter's embrace has already begun."

The ground cracked beneath them, and the wind howled again, more violently this time. The mountains trembled, the air thick with magic, as if the land itself was fighting against them. Lira's heart pounded in her chest as she raised her sword high, ready to face this new enemy, this darkness that had been hidden from them for so long.

But even as the battle began, even as the power of Ysra's magic collided with their own, Lira knew one thing to be true: the war was not over. The greatest battle was yet to come. The darkness that had been held back for so long was about to be unleashed.

And she and Eryn would have to face it together.

No matter the cost.

The wind howled around them, as if the mountains themselves were protesting the return of the darkness. The air felt thick, charged with an ancient energy, and Lira could feel the very earth beneath her feet trembling. The ground cracked and shifted, as if it too was torn between the warmth of the new world and the chilling pull of the old.

Ysra stood before them, the last remnants of her former self intertwined with the icy power she commanded. The magic in the air crackled, thick with anticipation. She raised her hands, and the wind spiraled into a vicious vortex around them, lifting the snow and sending it spiraling into the air. The ice at her feet cracked and broke, shards of frozen death scattering like daggers.

"You think you can stop me?" Ysra's voice was sharp, filled with both anger and something darker—something ancient, born of the mountains and the very cold that had suffocated Amara for centuries. "The barrier was never meant to be broken. You have no idea what you've unleashed."

Lira's heart thundered in her chest as the swirling wind clawed at her, threatening to throw her to the ground. She felt the cold seep into her bones, freezing her resolve. It was as if the very magic of the land was turning against them, trying to choke out the warmth they had fought so hard to create. The winter's embrace—the one they thought they had vanquished—was returning.

But Lira refused to back down. She stood firm, gripping her sword, the fire of her determination burning brighter than ever. "We've fought too hard, too long, for you to take this from us. The world is free. It is *ours* now. You won't bring it back into the darkness."

Eryn stepped forward, his eyes filled with the same fire. "Lira's right," he said, his voice low but filled with conviction. "The people of Amara will never return to the ice. We won't let you."

Ysra's lips curled into a cruel smile, her eyes glowing with an eerie light. She lowered her arms, and the wind stilled for a brief moment, leaving a suffocating silence in its wake. "You think you have the power to stop me? To undo what has been written in the bones of this world for millennia?"

Lira's heart skipped a beat. The weight of Ysra's words pressed down on her, her chest tightening with the fear of the unknown. What had they truly unleashed? What was it that they hadn't known—that they hadn't been told?

"The true darkness," Ysra continued, her voice a low whisper that seemed to echo in the empty air, "is not just the winter. It's the force that binds the seasons. Without the cold, without the balance of winter, there is nothing to hold the true chaos at bay. The ancient magic that we once controlled, that *I* once controlled, is the only thing keeping the darkness from consuming everything."

Lira's mind spun as she tried to grasp the magnitude of Ysra's words. They had always believed that winter was the enemy. That the curse, the eternal cold, was the thing they had fought to end. But now Ysra was telling them that winter was never the real danger. It had only been a barrier—one that had kept something much darker from consuming the world.

Eryn stepped closer to Lira, his hand tightening around hers. She could feel the heat of his determination flowing through their joined hands, grounding her, reminding her of everything they had already overcome.

"We've already freed the land," Eryn said, his voice a fierce challenge to Ysra. "We've already broken the chains that bound us. Whatever darkness you speak of—*we* can face it. The love we have, the world we've built, is stronger than anything you can threaten us with."

Ysra's eyes flared with a sudden, terrifying light. "You do not understand," she hissed, her voice rising in fury. "You cannot simply erase what has been written into the land. The magic of winter—of the seasons—is not a force to be ignored. You cannot change the cycles of life and death, of growth and decay, without consequences."

Lira swallowed hard, her mind racing. She had felt it—the force of the magic that still clung to the earth, even after the curse had been broken. It was not just the cold, but something deeper. Something tied to the fabric of the world itself. A balance that they had never fully understood, but had nonetheless disrupted when they shattered the eternal winter.

"What do you want?" Lira asked, her voice rising with the desperation of the question. "What will it take for you to stop this? You were the one who made the choice to keep us all in the cold. You're the one who bound us to this cursed magic. *You* broke the land! You've ruled through fear. And now you expect us to let you return to that?"

Ysra's face twisted with something dark, something cruel. "You broke the curse, yes," she said, her voice a low growl. "But in doing so, you broke the balance. The chaos is already rising, Lira. The land is already reacting to what you have done. The seasons have been interrupted. The cold may be gone for now, but without it, the true magic is collapsing. The darkness will return, and you will have no choice but to face it."

The ground beneath them began to shake once again, more violently this time. The mountains groaned, their peaks trembling as cracks began to form in the earth. The land, so recently healed, was now splitting apart, the deep fissures opening like gaping mouths. The wind picked up again, but this time it was more than just a cold breeze—it was a hurricane, a storm of rage and power that ripped through the air, sending debris flying.

"Eryn," Lira gasped, clutching his arm as the earth trembled beneath them. "What is happening?"

"It's the magic," Eryn said, his voice strained as he held her steady. "The seasons were never meant to be broken. The land... the world is reacting to the disruption. It's fighting back. We need to stop her. *Now.*"

But Ysra was already raising her hands, her face twisted with madness as she summoned the fury of the storm. The ice swirled around her, her power growing exponentially, filling the air with the scent of cold steel and ancient magic.

"*This* is the price of your choices," Ysra said, her voice ringing with a kind of triumph. "You will never be able to erase what has been done. The darkness is returning, and you, Lira, you and Eryn—your love, your sacrifice—will not be enough to stop it."

Lira felt a surge of power rise within her—a force she had never tapped into before, something deep within her that had been awakened by the broken curse, something tied to the very heart of Amara. The magic of the land had flowed through her, had fused with her soul when she made the sacrifice to break the curse. She had unlocked a power she didn't fully understand. But now, standing before Ysra, as the world seemed to crumble around them, Lira knew that this was the moment. This was the battle where she would have to face the very heart of the darkness she had unleashed.

"*We* are the change," Lira whispered, her voice filled with fire, her eyes locked on Ysra's. "And we *will* stop you."

Lira raised her sword, its blade glowing with the warmth of the land, the fire of her resolve, and the magic she had unlocked. The earth beneath her feet roared to life, the ground shifting as if in response to her will. Eryn's sword gleamed beside her, a symbol of their unity, of the love that had carried them through every trial, every battle, and every sacrifice.

Together, they surged forward, a single force of nature, determined to stop the return of the darkness.

The battle that followed was one of elemental fury—a clash of ice and fire, of magic and will, each strike shaking the very foundation of the world. The storm raged around them, the land trembling, the sky flashing with the fury of the gods themselves. Ysra's power surged, but Lira and Eryn stood firm, their swords cutting through the darkness, through the storm, determined to reclaim the land that was theirs.

And then, with one final, blinding flash of light, the storm broke.

The earth stilled, the air cleared. The mountains, once again, fell silent. Ysra crumbled to the ground, her power dissipating, her form unraveling as the last vestiges of the curse were broken. The land, the seasons, the magic—it all began to settle, the storm subsiding like the end of a long, violent storm.

Lira stood over the fallen remnants of the winter, her heart racing, her chest heaving with the weight of the battle. Eryn was beside her, his hand firmly on her shoulder, grounding her in the stillness that followed.

"We did it," Lira whispered, her voice shaking, barely believing the words that had escaped her lips.

The land, the world, was finally at peace. The darkness had been vanquished. The cold was gone for good.

And in its place, the warmth of spring, of love, of sacrifice, bloomed.

But Lira knew, as she turned to face Eryn, that their fight would never truly end. The world would continue to shift and change, but together, they would face whatever came next.

For as long as they had each other, nothing could ever break them.

The love they had shared, the love that had saved the world, would never fade. It would live on as the foundation of the new world they had built together.

The last winter's embrace had ended.

And with it, a new dawn had begun.

Twenty-One

The Final Dawn

The sky, once the color of ash and iron, was slowly, steadily, breaking apart. For the first time in centuries, the clouds above Amara parted, revealing the first true light that the land had seen since the curse was cast so long ago. The darkness, which had held sway over the land for as long as anyone could remember, was finally receding, its grip weakening as the sun climbed higher, shedding its golden light over the world.

Lira stood at the edge of a vast plain, her eyes fixed on the horizon, where the first rays of the new dawn were spilling over the mountains, illuminating the land in a brilliance that felt both familiar and foreign. She had seen the world through the cold, had lived through the endless winter, and now, as the warmth of spring touched the earth once more, it felt like the beginning of something new.

Beside her, Eryn stood, his hand resting lightly on her shoulder. They had been through so much together—so many battles, so many sacrifices—but now, there was only peace. The curse was lifted. The land was free. And the promise of a future, of a world without the darkness that had plagued them, lay before them, as boundless as the sky itself.

Lira closed her eyes for a moment, feeling the warmth of the sun on her face, the light of the new world brushing against her skin. It was a sensation she had not felt in so long—something she had almost forgotten was possible. The cold, the harsh winter that had shaped their lives and their struggles, was finally gone. It was not a fading memory, not something lingering in the background. It was *gone*.

"You did it," Eryn said quietly, his voice filled with awe as he watched the sun rise higher, bathing the land in its glow. "We did it."

Lira nodded, but her expression was unreadable, her thoughts far from the present moment. She had always believed that the moment they broke the curse would be the end of the fight. That once they had defeated the darkness, once the land was free, their struggles would be over. But now, as she stood there, the weight of what they had done seemed heavier than ever.

The sun's warmth was a balm to the soul, but it also brought with it an undeniable truth—something they had never fully grasped before. The curse was gone, yes. The land was free. But peace, true peace, was not something easily won. And even now, as the land basked in the light of the new dawn, Lira knew that their journey was far from over.

"What now?" she whispered, her voice barely audible, though Eryn heard her clearly.

He turned to her, his gaze steady and filled with the quiet strength that had carried them through every hardship. "Now," he said, his voice soft, "we live. We rebuild. We watch this new world grow."

Lira's heart tightened, and she shook her head. "It's not that simple. The darkness is gone, yes. But the scars remain. There are still forces in this world that are waiting for a chance to rise again."

Eryn's expression softened, but there was no fear in his eyes. Only the quiet certainty that had always defined him. "The darkness will never return, Lira. Not in the way it once did. You and I—we're proof of that. We've fought for the light. For love. For the world we wanted to see. And now that the curse is lifted, the world is ours to shape."

The weight of his words settled over her like a blanket, comforting yet heavy. She wanted to believe him, wanted to believe that everything they had fought for was enough, that the new world would flourish without the shadow of fear hanging over it. But there was something deeper inside her—something that had always felt tied to the land, to the magic, to the seasons—that told her the battle was not truly over.

The wind began to pick up, a light breeze at first, but then it started to grow stronger, carrying with it a whisper—soft, elusive, almost like a voice calling from the far reaches of time.

Lira's eyes narrowed as she turned her gaze toward the horizon, the sound of the wind mingling with something else. A low hum that seemed to come from the earth itself, a resonance that vibrated through the ground beneath her feet. The land was alive, yes, but there was something different about it now. Something stirring.

"What is that?" Lira asked, her voice a mix of awe and unease.

Eryn's brow furrowed as he turned toward the sound. "It's the land," he said, his voice steady. "The earth is still healing. It's a response to the magic we've unleashed."

But Lira felt something else. The hum in the air was not simply the earth healing—it was something more ancient. Something primordial. It felt like the pulse of the world itself, deep beneath the surface, like the beat of a heart that had not been felt in centuries.

The earth trembled again, this time more violently. The ground beneath them cracked, fissures opening in the earth as if the land was breathing—shifting, waking up from a long sleep.

"Eryn!" Lira's voice cracked as she stepped back, her eyes wide with realization. "It's not over. The magic—it's *changing.*

The earth trembled beneath their feet as Lira and Eryn surged forward, their swords raised, the power of the land itself surging through their veins. The Guardian of the Cycle, a being born of stone, ice, and ancient magic, loomed over them, its monstrous form casting a shadow that stretched across the land. Its eyes glowed with the fury of centuries, and its voice reverberated through the very air, shaking the ground beneath them.

"You cannot fight what you do not understand," the Guardian growled, its voice shaking the very air with ancient power. "The balance must be restored. Winter and summer. Night and day. Life and death. They are not just seasons—they are the forces that sustain this world. Without them, all will crumble."

Lira's heart raced, but her resolve only strengthened. She could feel the magic within her—the warmth of the sun, the fire of the land—and she knew that she would not let the Guardian reclaim the world they had fought so hard to save.

"We understand enough," Lira said, her voice cutting through the tension like the sharp edge of her blade. "We fought for the balance. We fought to end the tyranny of winter. We fought for freedom—for the people."

The Guardian's laugh was low and mocking, the sound like thunder in the sky. "Foolish children," it rumbled. "You think you have won. You think you have restored the balance. But you have only broken it. The chaos you unleashed is irreversible."

Lira's pulse raced, but she took a step forward, steadying herself. She felt Eryn's presence beside her, his strength, his unyielding resolve. Together, they were unstoppable.

"No," Eryn's voice rang out, sharp and clear. "You are wrong. We didn't break the balance—we were the ones who fought to restore it. We freed the land, yes. But the magic we released— the love that shaped this world—will never be undone."

The Guardian's eyes glowed brighter, its form shifting with an unnatural, otherworldly energy, as if it were drawing strength from the very chaos that it had warned them of. The ground beneath their feet cracked open, and the temperature dropped, the icy wind howling through the valley. The magic was palpable now, an oppressive force that threatened to consume everything in its path.

Lira and Eryn stood firm, their hearts aligned, their minds clear. They were not just fighting for themselves—they were fighting for the future. For the world they had already begun to rebuild. For the love they had found in each other, and for the people who had placed their trust in them.

Together, they raised their swords high, the weapons crackling with the magic of the land, the warmth of the sun. The Guardian swung its massive arm, sending waves of ice and wind crashing toward them, but Lira was faster. She moved with the swiftness of the wind, her sword flashing through the air as it met the Guardian's attack head-on, the force of the collision sending a shockwave through the earth.

Eryn was right behind her, his blade a blur of motion as he slashed through the creature's defenses. The Guardian's power surged, but the bond between Lira and Eryn was stronger. They were not just two individuals fighting together—they were one, their hearts and minds in perfect harmony. The magic of the land flowed through them both, fueling their every strike, their every movement.

With a final, coordinated strike, they pierced the Guardian's core. The world seemed to hold its breath, time itself slowing as the Guardian let out a roar of pain, its massive form shuddering as the magic holding it together began to unravel. The ground cracked beneath their feet, and the storm of ice and wind began to die down, the power of the Guardian faltering.

But even as the Guardian crumbled, the earth beneath them continued to tremble, the pulse of chaos still lingering, still trying to break free. Lira felt the magic of the world fighting to stay balanced, to maintain the equilibrium they had fought so hard to restore.

"This is not over," the Guardian's voice echoed, but it was weaker now, fading into the wind. "You have won… for now. But the balance can never be truly restored. Chaos will always return. It is only a matter of time."

Lira's breath caught in her throat as the last remnants of the Guardian faded into the air, its form dissolving into dust and ice. The winds stilled, the ground stopped shaking, and for a brief moment, all was silent.

Lira stood motionless, the weight of what had just transpired sinking in. They had defeated the Guardian. They had fought for the balance, for the future of the world, but the price of victory had been steep. The darkness had been powerful, more than they had ever realized. Yet, somehow, they had prevailed. The world they had fought for—this world—was theirs now.

But even as the final remnants of the battle faded away, Lira knew that peace would always be fragile. The balance was delicate, and it would require constant care, constant vigilance. The chaos that had once threatened the land would never fully be gone. But the magic that had shaped their world, that had given them the strength to fight, was something far stronger than any darkness that might come.

Eryn stepped beside her, his hand finding hers, his touch warm, grounding. He met her eyes, his gaze steady. "It's over," he said softly, as if saying it aloud might make it real.

Lira nodded slowly, her heart still racing from the battle, from the weight of what they had just faced. The final battle. The culmination of everything they had fought for. They had defeated the darkness—together.

But even in the quiet aftermath, as the sun rose higher and the warmth of the dawn washed over them, Lira couldn't shake the feeling that their journey was far from over. The world was free, yes. But it was still in its infancy. The seeds they had planted, the love they had fought to preserve, had only just begun to grow.

"We've done it, Eryn," Lira whispered, her voice thick with emotion, with exhaustion, but also with hope. "We've freed the land. But now… we rebuild."

Eryn squeezed her hand, a gentle smile tugging at the corner of his lips. "Together, we rebuild," he said, his voice strong, unwavering. "And we'll protect it. The love we've fought for will be the foundation of this new world."

The first true light of dawn washed over the land, turning the once-barren plains into a sea of golden warmth. The frost, the chill, the remnants of the darkness that had once defined their world, melted away in the light. It was a new beginning. A world free from the cold.

And as Lira looked up at the sun, she realized that, even though the battle had been hard, even though the cost had been great, the world they had fought for was now theirs to shape. Their love, their sacrifice, had laid the foundation for a future where warmth and light would always be present.

They had broken the cycle of winter and summer. They had broken the curse that had plagued the land for so long.

And with the final dawn, a new world began.

The world, at last, was theirs.

www.ingramcontent.com/pod-product-compliance
Lightning Source LLC
LaVergne TN
LVHW020734200726

843506LV00009B/736